# MARTIN de PORRES

## *A Saint of the Americas*

### A "15 DAYS OF PRAYER" BOOK

### BRIAN J. PIERCE, O.P.

Liguori

LIGUORI, MISSOURI

*Imprimi Potest:*
Richard Thibodeau, C.Ss.R.
Provincial, Denver Province
The Redemptorists

Published by Liguori Publications
Liguori, Missouri
www.liguori.org

**Library of Congress Cataloging-in-Publication Data**

Pierce, Brian J.
    Martin de Porres : a saint of the Americas / Brian J. Pierce.—1st ed.
      p. cm.
    "A 15 days of prayer book."
    Includes bibliographical references.
    ISBN 0-7648-1216-5
    1. Martin, de Porres, Saint, 1579–1639. 2. Christian saints—Prayer-books and devotions—English. I. Title.

BX4700.M397P54  2004
282'.092—dc22                                 2004048359

Printed in the United States of America
07 06 05 04 03   5 4 3 2 1
First edition

# MARTIN
# de PORRES

Also in the *15 Days of Prayer* collection:

# Table of Contents

# Introduction

MARTIN DE PORRES IS A SAINT for all peoples and all times. Not only was he a man of mixed blood, but his whole life was a great blending together of different colors and shapes—a brilliant kaleidoscope of loving kindness. Martin's life is a composite sketch of holiness, combining the apostolic zeal of Saint Dominic, the simple love for creation of Saint Francis of Assisi, and the endless compassion for the poor and sick of Blessed Teresa of Calcutta—all in one. Martin's life was a witness to ancient truths and traditional spiritual values, while at the same time bringing forth a new expression of the spiritual life: radical, simple, and holy. He had the gift of spontaneous joy, as well as a disarming capacity for turning suffering and oppression into an encounter with God.

Martin did not write any books or treatises or preach any sermons during his life. His life *was* his preaching, and a well-lived preaching at that. Though we do not have any of his own writings, we do have a vast number of testimonies of his saintly life, collected soon after his death from among his contemporaries. In a way similar to Mother Teresa of Calcutta, Martin's life of holiness and unconditional love of the poor was very well known during his own lifetime, so much so that it comes as a surprise that, *unlike* Mother Teresa, almost two hundred years had to pass before he was declared a blessed of the Church.

Known for his long hours of prayer and extreme penances, Martin also loved gardening and enjoyed a playful relationship with animals of all kinds. His purity of heart and inner freedom came together to form a man who was both spiritual seeker and witness to God's boundless love.

It was during the short papacy of Blessed John XXIII, the joyful prophet of Vatican II, that Martin was finally given his due recognition as a saint of the Church. Two years prior to the canonization, a group of 250 Peruvians had visited the pope to ask that Martin be elevated to the communion of saints. The Holy Father addressed the group that day, saying "I have thought of your lands, your immense and beautiful continent, lands where saints have flourished...humble, pure and innocent....Such was Martin de Porres, long recognized as blessed, but upon whose forehead we already see shining the radiant halo of the saints.... [Like them] it is necessary to always speak and practice the truth, to observe the virtue of justice for all people, doing harm to no one, and, above all, to establish a world of fraternal and universal love. This is the great triumph of the gospel, the purest flower of Christian civilization and culture."[1]

Two years later, on May 6, 1962—springtime in Rome—before a crowd of more than forty thousand persons from all corners of the globe, the Holy Father Pope John XXIII said of Martin, the patron saint of social justice, "A springtime flower has opened in the Church."[2] What fitting words, spoken by a holy man and at a moment in the Church's history in which a springtime breeze was ushering in a new era of the Spirit. We can only pray that the beauty and the sweet fragrance of Martin's gospel-centered life continue today to spread throughout the world.

*Finally I would like to add a personal note. I, like my brother, Martin, am a Dominican friar. Before I was a Dominican friar, though, I was "just Brian" who, as a seventeen-year-old, found myself living as a high-school foreign exchange student in Peru, Martin's homeland. Eight years later, during the course of my theological studies as a Dominican, I was again privileged to study* theology for a year in Peru, this time living in a Dominican community next door to the small room where Martin was born in Lima. Each day we joined the friars in the Priory of Santo Domingo (a few blocks away) for our noon meal—the very convento where Martin lived out his forty-five years of Dominican life. I have spent many hours snooping around and praying in many of Martin's secret hideouts! I am quite certain that, along with the loving support of my family and friends, it is because of Saint Martin that I am a Dominican today.

Most of my ministry as a Dominican friar has been in Latin America—principally in Honduras. I can say without a doubt that it is the poor of Latin America who have evangelized my heart and taught my soul to trust in God. At the age of seventeen, as I looked upon the violence of poverty and oppression for the first time in my life, I knew I would never be the same. The faces, the eyes, and the smiles of the people I have known throughout Latin America, despite their struggles, have shown me the face of the God, whose love endures forever. I knew I would never be the same, and I hope I never will be. I thank God for this most wonderful gift.

I was invited to undertake this writing project during the twentieth year of my profession as a Dominican friar in the Province of Saint Martin de Porres. In fact, I began my Dominican life as a novice in the community and parish of Saint Martin de Porres in Columbia, South Carolina. Something tells me this was part of God's plan "in the beginning." I am grateful to Liguori Publications for this sacred opportunity; to my friend, Beth Clary, for her wise help and encouragement; and to the sisters at the Forest of Peace Ashram for a quiet place to write. Above all, I thank my Dominican brothers and sisters who have gifted me during these many years with their faithful love, and who have entrusted me with Saint Dominic's passion for "the holy preaching."

Our Dominican province was founded in 1979 to bring about "a new birth in hope" in eleven of the southern states in the United States. Conscious of the large Black and growing Latino popula-

*tions in the South, the founding friars chose to place our province under the patronage of Saint Martin de Porres. This year—2004— we celebrate our twenty-fifth anniversary as a province. I pray to Martin, "Martincito," my beloved friend and brother, that he continue to walk this paschal journey with us and with the people of God throughout the world—leading us all home to God's promised land of justice, joy, and lasting peace.*

## NOTES

1. Pope John XXIII, cited in Guillermo Alvarez, O.P., *Historia de la Orden Dominicana en el Peru,* vol. III (Lima: Dominicans of Peru, 1999), pp. 309–311.
2. *Ibid.,* p. 347.

# A Brief Chronology of Saint Martin de Porres' Life

MARTIN DE PORRES WAS BORN into a world that was changing at a record pace. It was also a world in turmoil. Though he was a native of Peru, a country that runs along the Pacific coast of South America, neither of Martin's parents was born in Peru. One could say that Martin knew what it felt like to live in exile from the day of his birth.

During the second half of the sixteenth century, Peru was just beginning to dig its way out from the ashes of the darkest night of its history—*la noche oscura de la conquista*—the Inca Empire's dark night of conquest. One day, a ship, flying the flag of Spain, landed on the coast of Peru's ancient lands, and the next day the peoples who lived there were the private property of a foreign power. Martin de Porres was born into a world that worshiped the unholy trinity of power, violence, and gold.

It was not an easy time to be born in Peru. For the native indigenous peoples it was hell; they lost everything overnight—most importantly, their sacred lands and their sovereignty. The only thing worse than being a conquered Indian was to be an African slave. Martin was the son of a freed African slave. Freed, yet not free. How free could the daughter of African slaves be in a land that was occupied militarily by the very same nation that had dragged her parents from Africa to a life in chains on the other side of the ocean? It was worse than hell.

God cannot be chained by human hatred, though, and it is because of God that we have Saint Martin de Porres. Martin's whole life reads almost like sacred Scripture—a retelling of the Exodus story. Martin is Israel, and his life is the story of a people's journey from slavery and exile into a land of promise, a land flowing with milk and honey. And to the extent that we are on a journey to a fuller and freer life, it is our story, too.

Most important of all, though, is that Martin's story—like Israel's—is God's story. It is a story about faithfulness and love. The story line is simple and has three acts: (1) an illegitimate mulatto baby is born in a conquered colony of Spain; (2) as a child, he falls in love with God and with the poor; (3) Martin becomes a Dominican brother and dies a holy man at the age of sixty. It is so simple that it almost seems unbelievable. But it is a true story—beautifully true.

But lest we get ahead of ourselves, let us begin where the story begins: in Lima, Peru, in the year of our Lord 1579.

## HIS LIFE[1]

**1579:** Probably sometime in November or December, Martin was born in Lima, Peru. The exact date is not known, though often the date of his baptism is given as his birth date. He was the son of a Spanish *hidalgo* named Juan de Porras (or Porres) and a freed Creole-Black woman from Panama named Ana Velásquez.

**December 9, 1579:** Martin was baptized in the Church of San Sebastián in Lima by Father Juan Antonio Polanco.

**1586:** Martin and his younger sister, Juana, were taken by their father to Guayaquil, Ecuador, where Juan de Porras had a government job. It is not known why Ana, their mother, was left behind. Martin lived about a year in Guayaquil, probably studying, while Juana remained there several years with the family of Diego Marcos de Miranda, relatives of Juan.

**1587 to 1594**: From approximately the age of eight until his entrance into the Dominican Order at the age of fifteen, Martin lived in Lima, in the poor, mostly African and Creole neighborhood of Malambo, near the San Lázaro Hospital, in the home of Isabel García Michel. Though it seems that Martin had regular contact with his mother during these years, it can only be guessed that it was for economic reasons that Juan de Porras arranged for his son to live elsewhere. It was also during these years that Martin apprenticed as both an herbalist/pharmacist and as a barber and minor surgeon.

**1591**: It is very probable that sometime during this year Martin received the sacrament of confirmation, anointed with the holy oil by Archbishop Toribio Alfonso de Mogrovejo, a well-known defender of the rights of the conquered indigenous peoples and later himself declared a saint of the Church. It is believed that Martin's mother accompanied him for his confirmation.[2]

**1594**: Martin de Porres entered the Priory of Our Lady of the Holy Rosary (also called the Convento de Santo Domingo, after the Order's founder, Saint Dominic of Guzmán). Martin's aim was to live the rest of his life as a *donado*—an oblate brother attached to the Order, but without religious vows. It is probable that sometime during this year he was given the habit of the *donado* brother: a white tunic, a black cape, a hat to protect him from the hot sun (which Martin apparently never wore), and a string of rosary beads that hung around his neck.

**June 2, 1603**: Martin de Porres professed his solemn religious vows and promised obedience for the rest of his life in the hands of Father Alonso de Sea, subprior of the community. He also made vows of chastity and poverty, signing the priory's Book of Profession in his own hand as "Brother Martín de Porras."

**1594 to 1639**: Martin de Porres lived out his life of holiness and service as a Dominican brother in the same priory where he entered at age fifteen.

**November 3, 1639**: Brother Martin de Porres died, surrounded by his community, after a short illness, probably typhus. He was sixty years old and had lived forty-five years as a Dominican.

**November 4, 1639**: Martin was buried beneath the Chapter Hall of the Priory after a day in which thousands of devoted friends, rich and poor, black, white, Indian and *mestizo,* came to pay their last respects to their beloved apostle of charity.

**1660**: Peter de Villagómez, Archbishop of Lima, opened the process of collecting the depositions regarding Martin's virtues and sanctity of life. Many of his closest friends and companions, still alive at the time, were able to give personal accounts of his remarkable life.

**October 29, 1837**: Martin de Porres was beatified by Pope Gregory XVI, almost two hundred years after his death, and one week after the beatification of his close friend and Dominican confrere, Juan Macías.

**May 6, 1962**: Martin was canonized a saint by Pope John XXIII.

## NOTES
1. A number of the details of Martin's life are taken from Juan Antonio del Busto, JAB.
2. JAB, p. 60.

# Abbreviations and Main Sources Used in This Book

O.P.  refers to a member of the Order of Preachers, commonly known as the Dominicans.

JAB  Juan Antonio del Busto Duthurburu, *San Martín de Porras* (Lima: Pontificia Universidad Católica del Peru), 1992. Translations by Brian J. Pierce, O.P.

AGR  Alex García-Rivera, *St. Martin de Porres: The "Little Stories" and the Semiotics of Culture* (New York: Orbis Books), 1995.

CAV  Giuliana Cavallini, *Saint Martin de Porres: Apostle of Charity* (Rockford, Ill.: TAN Books and Publishers, Inc.), 1979.

BBS  Bruce B. Schultz, O.P., "Retrieving the African Roots of San Martín de Porras." This is a yet-to-be-published thesis.

It is a shame that there has not been more written about Martin de Porres. Most of the writings have been devotional, and often for a children's audience. The book by José Antonio del Busto Duthurburu, cited frequently in these pages, is probably the newest and best *history* of Martin's life. Though the book was written only in 1992 (in Spanish), it is presently out of print. Giuliana Cavallini's book, though more devotional, does a nice job connecting Martin's life with the social and historical context in which he lived.

The most innovative and theologically stimulating book on Martin is the one by Alex García-Rivera. He has broken new ground by uncovering the deeper theological and spiritual levels of symbolic meaning in the many stories told of Martin's life, the so-called "little stories." His book is *St. Martín de Porres: The "Little Stories" and the Semiotics of Culture*, and is well worth reading. It is *not* a devotional book, however, and must be approached from both a scholarly and creative point of view. (Semiotics is defined as an analysis of systems of communication, including language, gestures, clothing, and so on.) The "little stories" of Martin (as is true with other saints) are often dismissed as cute little children's stories—flowery anecdotes of an equally flowery life. This dismissal is a great tragedy, and in Martin's case has only furthered what Bruce Schultz, O.P., calls the "infantalizing" of Martin.[1]

García-Rivera has rescued these stories from the dusty shelves of pious history and breathed new life into them. His work is too detailed to explain extensively here, but suffice it to say that the "little stories" told of Martin are filled with the "big stuff" we call the gospel of Jesus Christ. They are stories told from the underside of history, and because of that, they tend to turn things upside down in order to help us see life with new eyes. Hopefully, the fifteen reflections in this book will give the reader a taste of the spiritual power contained in these "little stories."

## NOTES

1. Bruce B. Schultz, O.P., "Retrieving the African Roots of San Martín de Porras." This dissertation has yet to be published.

## ONE

# From Chaos to Compassion

### FOCUS: THE BEGINNINGS

Martin de Porres' childhood had its share of chaos. Not only was this true within his own family, but Martin's whole world was struggling daily with the dehumanizing reality of material poverty, intensified by the violence of living in a country under foreign domination. What is amazing, though, when one looks back at Martin's difficult beginnings, is that he allowed God to transform his childhood chaos and poverty into compassion. In other people, these same ingredients would have resulted in a life of bitterness and anger. But Martin gave it all to God, who took the Spanish and African threads of his fragile heart and wove them into a beautiful tapestry of divine love (Ps 139:13).

*The exact date of Martin de Porres' birth is not known. What is known, though, is that Martin was baptized in the Church of San Sebastián in Lima, Peru, on December 9, 1579. The baptismal*

*registry reads: "On Wednesday, the ninth of December 1579, I
baptized Martin, son of an unknown father and of Ana Velásquez
a free black woman. The godparents were Juan de Bribiesca and
Ana de Escarcena. I have signed this: —Juan Antonio Polanco."*[1]

## "SOMETHING BEAUTIFUL FOR GOD"

And thus begins our magnificent story. With just a few words, we
already have a glimpse into the unique life of Martin, who came
into this world already touched by suffering. One cannot help
but hear echoes of the poor, humble birth of Jesus, his parents
turned away from the inn in Bethlehem, leaving Jesus himself
with "nowhere to lay his head" (Mt 8:20). Martin was probably
just a day or two old at the time of his baptism, as this was the
custom of the time. Ana, his mother, with the support of the godparents, had to take full responsibility for Martin's baptism and
early childhood. She arrived at the church of San Sebastián that
December day a poor, freed Creole-Black slave,[2] and now, on top
of everything else, a single mother. As we look back several centuries later, we see her story reflected in the stories of many people
of our own day. She had very little support except her faith in
God.

History later fills in more of the details of Martin's humble
beginnings. His mother had come from Panama; given the laws
of the day, we know that she would have been freed from slavery
either by paying for her freedom herself or by having been granted
it by her slave owner.[3] What is significant for us to keep in mind,
though, is that Martin's mother had once been a slave, a key piece
of the story when one considers the whole scope of Martin's life
and commitment to the poor. This also means that Martin, the
mulatto saint from Peru, had the blood of African slaves running
through his veins. His life carried within it the story of his ancestors. Martin's soul never ceased being African.

Just as significant as his African heritage—at least in terms of molding Martin during his early years—was the Spanish side of his life. The baptismal annotation, "son of an unknown father," put Martin into the category of an illegitimate child. In sixteenth-century Catholicism, this was no easy label to live with. Says Alex García-Rivera, "Juan condemned his son to illegitimacy, a serious consequence in the strictly hierarchical society of Lima."[4] Juan de Porras (or Porres)[5] was a Spaniard, a descendant from a long line of *hidalgos*—Christian warriors whose lives were pledged to the Spanish Crown. José Antonio del Busto has reconstructed what seems to be the family tree of Martin's father, all the way back to the year 1102. If the proposed genealogy is correct, Juan de Porras was the son of Martín de Porras y Santo Domingo and Isabel de la Peña, whose family was from Burgos in the Castille region of Spain. It also seems that our own Brother Martin had an uncle who was a Jesuit (named Martin also) and two aunts, Mariana and Jerónima, who were nuns.[6]

The *hidalgos* were elite soldiers, highly respected within the empire, though they were not nobility, as some have concluded. Their greatest honor was to die in war. The *hidalgo* was also expected to live a chaste life of continence, part of his honorary commitment to the king. That means that Juan's fathering of a son—especially with a freed slave woman of African descent—would have been considered a cause of shame. Rather than courageously admit that the dark-skinned son was his own, Juan chose instead to play it safe and distance himself from the family. Though he did appear once or twice, showing some interest in the lives of Martin and his younger sister, Juana, his overall commitment to Ana and the children was negligent at best. Juan took both children to Ecuador in 1586, apparently with the intention of providing the two with an education. Juana remained in Ecuador, while Martin returned to Lima about a year later, and was given over to the care of a woman named Isabel García Michel. It is not known why he did not return to live with his mother upon returning to Lima.

We can only imagine to what extent Martin's relationship

with his cowardly father left an empty wound in his heart. He does seem to have been able to give his wounded heart over to God, though, who transformed the suffering and shame into compassion and love. In a strange way, Martin's heart did finally become something like the warrior heart of his father's side of the family, but in a different way. Rather than give his heart in loyalty to the king of Spain, Martin gave his heart to God's kingdom of love and justice. It was precisely the coming together in Martin of his African soul and his Spanish warrior's heart that molded him into God's troubadour of compassion.

It is a common error to elevate saints to a level of holiness that makes them seem more divine than human. While this is a natural tendency when one considers a life like Martin's, we do ourselves a disservice if we forget the human side of their lives. This is especially true in Martin's case. Martin was born into a very difficult social situation. About forty years before his birth (1533), Peru's Incan emperor, Atahualpa, was assassinated by Juan Pizarro and the entire Incan empire was conquered by the Spanish army. Almost overnight, the *conquistadores* reduced to slavery a people who had been free for centuries. Dominican friar, Bartolomé de las Casas, writing just before the time of Martin's birth, spoke of seeing the indigenous peoples of the Americas "beaten, afflicted, insulted and crucified [like Christ] by those Spaniards who destroy and ravage the Indians" in their greedy pursuit of gold and power.[7] Martin's father, we must remember, was a representative of this brutal and unjust structure of conquest and greed.

To make matters worse, notes Cyprian Davis, O.S.B., a black Catholic historian, "In the sixteenth century a Spaniard would have believed that a war with the Moslems was always justified. Black Africans were seen as inhabitants of Moslem territory. Hence, they could be enslaved."[8] Peru brought together the worst of both worlds: conquered Indians and enslaved Africans.[9] This was the world Martin was born into. What could it have possibly felt like for Martin, who was a dark-skinned mulatto,[10] to have a mother who was a freed black slave and a father who was part of the army of white conquerors that was now trafficking in African slaves? It is unimaginable.

It is important for us to *feel* the social hell that Martin was born into. We simply perpetuate the injustice if all we do is look back and admire beautiful little Martin with his broom in hand, sweeping the corridors of the Dominican cloister with an angelic face. Martin was born into the violence of war and oppression. He was one of society's rejects, and his own father—at least for a large part of his life—preferred to protect his own honor rather than offer protection and a last name to his newborn son.

It is a rather tragic picture until one looks into the heart and soul of God's beloved son, Martin, and glimpses with awe that springtime flower as it blossoms in the midst of a foul heap of rubbish. Martin allowed God to redeem what must have seemed an irredeemable situation. In the words of Mother Teresa of Calcutta, Martin, rooted in faith, decided very early on to make of his life "something beautiful for God." And God "saw that it was good" (Gen 1:12).

## REFLECTION QUESTIONS

What do I experience in my heart and soul when I look back at the painful beginnings of Martin's life? Do I tend to forget that the saints lived in worlds and struggled with difficulties as real as our own? Where do I see the violence of war, oppression and racism still alive today? Do I have any past family issues for which I, like Martin, long for healing? Am I inspired to make my life "something beautiful for God" just as Martin did? How might I take a step in that direction today?

## NOTES

1. JAB, p. 38.
2. A Creole-Black was one who had been born in America, of African parents.
3. There is some speculation that Ana's family came from the northwest coast of the African continent, near the Senegal River (JAB, p. 46). More investigation needs to be undertaken in this area, some of which will hopefully be clarified with the publication of a dissertation by Bruce B. Schultz, O.P.
4. Alex García-Rivera, St. Martin de Porres: The "Little Stories" and the Semiotics of Culture (New York: Orbis Books, 1995), pp. 2–3.
5. The family name "de Porres" is also rendered frequently as "de Porras." We know that Martin signed his own name at least once as "Brother Martin de Porras." His family used both versions interchangeably. We have chosen "de Porres" since it is the more common spelling, and the one used in the official canonization documents. See JAB, pp. 39–42 and BBS.
6. JAB, pp. 39–42.
7. Bartolomé de las Casas, History of the Indies, translated and edited by Andrée Collard (New York: Harper and Row, 1971), III, pp. 264–265.
8. Cyprian Davis, O.S.B., The History of Black Catholics in the United States (New York: Crossroad, 1990), pp. 22–33.
9. It is estimated that in the year of Martin's birth, 1579, there were about four thousand African slaves in Lima. By 1614, Lima had a population of a little more than twenty-five thousand inhabitants, and almost eleven thousand of these were African or mulatto. This was almost half of the city's population. See Noé Zevallos, Rosa de Lima: Compromiso y Contemplación (Lima: CEP, 1988), pp. 2–3; 35–36. See also JAB, pp. 24–25.
10. A mulatto is a person of mixed (black and white/Spanish) race.

## TWO

# Christ Crucified

### FOCUS: SOLIDARITY IN PAIN

Given the difficult beginnings of Martin's life, one can understand how the cross of Christ became such a central part of his spirituality. Even to this day, the crucified Christ continues to be a popular devotion for many of the poor of Latin America. Unfortunately, this spiritual link to the cross of Christ is misunderstood by many, dismissed as just one more way that the poor passively allow themselves to remain oppressed. Nothing could be further from the truth. For Martin de Porres, it was through Christ crucified that the God of salvation drew near to his pain, bringing hope through the solidarity of love.

*Martin asked Isabel García for a wax candle, or a stub of one....Afraid of a fire, but mostly wanting to know what was happening, Isabel allowed herself to be tempted by curiosity. Drawing near to the young boy's room, she peered through the cracks in the door. What she saw deeply moved her. Martin was on his knees, quiet, silent, and praying before an image of the Crucified. His dark silhouette was piously outlined against the glow of the candle, and such was this scene of prayerful anointing that it seemed almost impossible for such a young child.*[1]

## APOSTLE OF COMPASSION

It was at Isabel García's house, where Martin had gone to live when he returned after a year in Guayaquil, Ecuador, that his daily prayer encounter with the crucifix began to take place.[2] Martin was probably about eight or nine at the time, and Doña Isabel's curiosity was roused when the young boy began asking for a candle each night before going to bed. After discovering the scene herself, she shared it with her daughter, Francisca, through whom the testimony eventually was added to those collected for the process of Martin's beatification.

What was it that drew Martin to the cross? What did he see in the crucified Christ that so deeply touched him? An eight-year-old boy might "play church" once or twice, but this was more than that. Might it be that Jesus became the tangible father figure that Martin never really had, or even a kind of older brother?

The crucifixes in Lima at the time would have been made by Spanish artisans or by local Peruvian woodworkers who copied the Spanish style. This means that the corpses nailed to the crucifixes were typically Spanish—a common trait in all of the early colonial religious art in America. That is very likely what caught Martin's attention. Here was this gentle Jesus, a white Spanish-looking Jesus, hanging helplessly, yet peacefully on the cross. His face, though marked by suffering, was also loving and compassionate—so different from many of the Spanish soldiers and colonists in Lima at the time. There was no violence in this Christ. He did not kill or oppress anyone, but instead gave his life for all. His love brought an end to violence. It was he, after all, who had prayed from the cross, "Father, forgive them, for they know not what they do."

This loving Christ, who had suffered in ways very similar to what Martin witnessed every day, spoke profoundly to him. Their quiet conversations each evening, illumined by the flame from the candle, laid a foundation for contemplative prayer that remained with Martin the rest of his life. Like Jesus, he too wanted to be an apostle of peace in a world so marked by violence.

For as long as he could remember, Martin had seen African and Incan slaves chained together and being led through the streets of Lima to be sold to Spanish colonists for work in the gold and silver mines.[3] He must have had heard many of his mother's stories about Panama and about his grandparents being brought over like animals in a ship from Africa. The Malambo district, where Martin lived with Mrs. García for seven years, is where the *corralones* were. "These were fenced-in areas, guarded by dogs, where the Africans, who had recently arrived from across the ocean, lived in huts…and waited to be sold or auctioned off publicly."[4] What went through Martin's mind as he passed by these cages, filled with human beings, we can only imagine.

For a young boy with the sensitivity that was so characteristic of Martin, no one could understand his heart's pain like the crucified Christ. When Martin was laughed at or spit at in the streets, called a *perro mulato* ("mulatto dog"), it was only the gentle, loving Christ on the cross who gave him solace and hope: "Be not afraid, I am with you." For the poor of Latin America, beaten and "crucified" during the years of Spanish and Portuguese colonial rule—and even into our own day—the bloodied corpse of the crucified Savior is, ironically, a great source of hope. They know that if God's beloved Son suffered in the same way as they do, then they are not alone; God is with them. In the words of martyred Salvadoran archbishop, Oscar Romero:

> We experience in the Christ of holy week, carrying his cross, that these are our people carrying their cross. We

experience in the Christ whose arms are open and crucified, our own crucified people. But it is from Christ that
our crucified and humiliated people find their hope.[5]

God is no stranger to suffering. For the poor, the crucified
Christ is the promised Emmanūel, the God who is with us—
always—no exceptions.[6]

There was in Lima, during Martin's lifetime, an image of the
crucified Christ that had been painted onto a wall in a neighborhood populated by Africans, very likely Malambo. This icon of
Christ was much revered by the poor in Martin's day. We do not
know exactly when it was painted, but we do know that the paint-
ing was miraculously saved from destruction during the terrible
earthquake of 1655, turning it into the most venerated sacred
symbol in all of Peru. Because of this miraculous event, the icon
became known as *El Señor de los Milagros* ("The Lord of
Miracles"). This image of Christ crucified continues to this day
to offer guidance, consolation, and hope for millions of Peruvians.[7]

Though we cannot know for sure, we can guess that Martin
was familiar with the icon of *El Señor de los Milagros*, and we
can imagine him praying quietly before the image in the neighborhood of Malambo, asking for solace and healing from the
sufferings of daily life. He probably wept when his own feelings
of neglect and rejection seemed to overwhelm him. But he knew
that he did not weep alone. Jesus wept with him. They shared a
common experience of suffering, and that made the friendship
even greater.[8]

When Martin entered the Dominican Order a few years later,
he again had to come face to face with suffering, this time due to
racist Church laws that sought to keep blacks and Indians from
becoming religious and priests.[9] One such law stated that "nowhere in the provinces of the Indies may there ever be received
into the holy habit and profession of our Order those known as
*mestizos* or those who are begotten on either side of their parents

of Indian or African blood."[10] These laws, however, could not undo the inner liberation which God had been working in Martin from his childhood days. His many years of tears before the crucifix of his gentle Jesus had already begun to shepherd his heart from wound to wonder, from slavery to solidarity. Martin's contemplation of the gentle face of Christ had revealed to him one of the greatest miracles of all—the beauty of his own face, the beauty of his own heart and soul. Like Jesus, Martin finally came to know that he, too, was an image of God, and that his heart was the temple of the Holy Spirit (1 Cor 3:16). Outward oppression can surely be unbearable, but the miracle of freedom that God gives in the temple of the human heart can never be taken away. Martin spent the rest of his life helping others to discover this great miracle, as well.

## REFLECTION QUESTIONS

Do I experience the miracle of God's love in my life? Spend some time in the coming days praying before an image of the crucified Christ. What word do I hear from the gentle Christ? Is there some personal or global suffering that I want to place into the hands of Jesus? Do I trust how deeply Jesus understands the pain? Do I see how many people today continue to be "crucified" by hatred in our world? What can I do to make a difference? Write a prayer to Christ on the cross.

## NOTES

1. JAB, p. 59.
2. It does seem that Martin had contact with his mother during these years and, though no one knows for certain, it may be that his father put him under the care of Isabel García because he did not think that Ana, his mother, had enough economic stability to care for the children.
3. Martin's home for the first eight years of his life was on Espíritu

Santo Street, the principal road connecting the Peruvian port
of Callao with the city of Lima. It was the road by which the
viceroy (a person appointed to govern a country or province
as a representative of the king of Spain) passed with his royal
entourage whenever he arrived or left the city. It was also the
"way of the cross" for the African slaves who were unloaded
at the port and led—handcuffed and chained together at the
neck—on their way to be sold in the Malambo neighborhood
(JAB, p. 37).

4. JAB, p. 58. Martin lived in the Malambo neighborhood (which
still exists today) roughly from 1587 to 1597, the year he
entered the Dominican priory.

5. Archbishop Oscar Romero, *Dia a Dia con Monseñor Romero*
(San Salvador: Publicaciones Pastorales del Arzobispado,
1999), p. 79.

6. Brian J. Pierce, O.P., "The Cross and the Crib: Hope From
the Underside," *America* (April 2, 1994), pp. 13–14. Isaiah
the prophet promised the coming of one named Emmanūel,
(Isa 7:14).

7. During the month of October, the month dedicated to the
Lord of Miracles, tens of thousands of Peruvians form pro-
cessions on different days and parade through the streets of
Lima to express their love and devotion for Christ, as he is
depicted in this icon. The image is popularly known as the
*Cristo morado* because it is draped in a bright purple cloth.
In honor of the image, thousands of Peruvians dress in purple
throughout the month of October.

8. Brian J. Pierce, O.P., "Martin de Porres: Compassion in Full
Bloom," *Justice, Peace & Dominicans: 1216–2001* (Dublin:
Dominican Publications, 2001), pp. 118–124.

9. Guillermo Alvarez, O.P., has written a fine history of the Order
and the Church in colonial Peru: *Historia de la Orden
Dominicana en el Peru*, three volumes (Dominicans of Peru,
1997 and 1999). On the question of racism, he writes that
Saint Rose of Lima (Martin's contemporary) "chose not to be

a cloistered nun simply because the racial segregation in the monasteries was a sign contrary to the gospel, a reason for scandal,'" cited in Noé Zevallos, *Rosa de Lima: Compromiso y Contemplación* (Lima: CEP, 1988), pp. 35–36. See also AGR, pp. 4–8, 108.

10. Stephen Clissold, *The Saints of South America* (London: Charles Knight & Co. Ltd., 1972), p. 63, as cited in BBS. The unpublished research of Bruce Schultz, O.P., in this area is quite extensive.

## THREE

# Brother to All

## FOCUS: ENTERING THE DOMINICANS

In 1594, at age fifteen, Martin knocked on the door of the Dominican Priory of Our Lady of the Rosary and asked to be received as a *donado*, a nonprofessed oblate brother. From the house where he lived in Malambo, Martin could hear the Dominican friars chanting the psalms in Latin. Those ancient songs, originally sung by a people freed from slavery, touched a deep core within young Martin. He spent the rest of his life as a member of this community—a friar preacher in the Order of Saint Dominic.[1] These years, filled with prayer, community, tireless service to the poor, and deep and lasting friendships, transformed him. He had finally found a family where he felt at home. The word *friar* (*fraile* in Spanish) comes from the Latin *frater*, meaning "brother." This was one of Martin's greatest gifts—he was truly a *brother* to all.

*One day, one of the friars saw Martin cleaning the toilets of the priory. During those days Martin had been staying at the house of the Archbishop of Mexico, who had come to Peru expressly to seek healing from Martin. The friar asked Martin, "Brother Martin, is it not better to be in the house of the Lord Archbishop of Mexico than in the toilets of the convent?" Martin quoted from one of the psalms, "I would rather be a doorkeeper in the house of my God / than live in the tents of wickedness" (84:10). He then added his own paraphrase, "Father Juan, I prefer a little time spent in this work than many days spent in the house of the Lord Archbishop."[2]*

## A SERVANT OF THE COMMUNITY

Brother Martin lived his Dominican life with such utter transparency that it often caught people off guard. The very presence of this young mulatto, son of an illegitimate union, was a bit of a question mark for many of the friars. He did not fit into any category, and this made some of them uncomfortable. Martin did not seem too bothered, though; he had already come to the realization that God frequently turns things upside down, disrupting the comfortable in order to reveal something new. Had not the Virgin Mary sung of that very thing many centuries before? "He [the Mighty One] has brought down the powerful from their thrones, / and lifted up the lowly; / he has filled the hungry with good things, / and sent the rich away empty" (Lk 1:52–53). God was used to turning things upside down. Martin was just the latest actor on God's stage.

The story of Martin's preferring the convent toilets over the house of the archbishop must be read in this *turning-things-upside-down* context. It is a perfect example of the "little stories" told of Martin; they are meant to shake us up a bit and challenge us to a more authentic living of the gospel. For Martin, there was no real difference between cleaning the toilets or tending to the needs of the sick archbishop. Father Juan, on the other hand, asked him the question, because he, evidently, considered it of much more value to be in the luxurious home of the archbishop than among smelly convent toilets. Martin's response (which had little to do with the spirituality of cleaning toilets) was intended to coax Father Juan into reflecting on his own priorities in life. This was the *earthiness* so characteristic of Martin. He lived fully in the present moment with a calm equanimity, not terribly concerned with what everyone else thought about his spiritual life. This gave him a groundedness which helped him remain anchored both in God and in the very real world of the poor.

This groundedness and balance were probably learned gradually during Martin's first years in the priory. It is quite likely, given his difficult childhood, that Martin would have had to struggle at first with the adjustment to living a life in community. He had *not* grown up in an environment in which he felt himself an equal to others, and that inner wound needed the healing balm of love, the experience of being accepted by his brother Dominicans.

We know that Martin entered the Order first as a *donado*. There seems to be reason to believe that, at least in the beginning, he felt himself unworthy to be a full-fledged, professed friar in the community. His self-image had been damaged by life's rough edges. What is marvelous, though, is to look back and see how Martin opened himself to God and allowed God to show him the way back home to the fullness of his human dignity. "Becoming a brother is more than joining a community," notes Timothy Radcliffe, O.P., "[It] will ask of me a patient and, sometimes painful, transformation of who I am."[3] Once Martin let God touch and transform the depth of his heart and soul, and discover there the gift of unconditional love, he was unstoppable. Like a springtime flower that breaks through the rain-softened ground, Martin sprouted and grew gracefully into "the freedom of the... children of God" (Rom 8:21). His life teaches all of us how to be brothers and sisters to one another.

One thing that probably did give Martin a big boost during

his first years in the priory was the joy of finding another mulatto brother like himself in the community. Miguel de Santo Domingo, originally from Cusco and also remembered for exemplary holiness, had also entered the Order as a *donado*, though by the time Martin entered in 1594, Miguel had already been professed as a lay brother.[4] Even though the racist environment within the colonial Church was quite severe, it does seem that the Dominicans in Peru were willing to break the laws when necessary, as the cases of both Miguel and Martin show.

The Dominican historian, Juan Meléndez, writing not long after Martin's death, relates a story about the sudden reappearance of Martin's father in his son's life. According to the story, Juan de Porras showed up at the priory one fine day (probably in 1596, two years after Martin entered) to protest his son's second-class citizenship in the community, demanding that Martin be allowed to make profession as a lay brother.[5] Giuliana Cavallini sheds light on the incident, noting that "Martin firmly refused" to acquiesce to his father's protests, since they "were inspired only by wounded pride and vainglory."[6] This explains the lapse of time between Juan de Porras' sudden foray into the life of a son whom he barely knew, and Martin's eventual acceptance of the community's invitation to become a solemnly professed brother. Martin *was* finally professed—seven years later—this time, though, as a free response to the love he had received from his *new* family, his brothers in Saint Dominic. The date was June 2, 1603, and the event was recorded with Martin's very own signature in the priory's Book of Professions.[7]

For Martin, there was really no difference between being a *donado* or a professed brother. He had given his life to God at a very young age, and so the day he knocked on the priory door in 1594, he simply continued the giving away of his life, this time to the brothers in his community and from there to the whole world. He never wavered. His entire life was a testimony of what it means to be a *brother*—following in the footsteps of Jesus, "the first-born within a large family" (Rom 8:29).

Humble as he was, Martin never lost his sense of humor. The religious habit worn by the *donados* and the habit worn by the professed brothers was not the same. There are references of his continuing to wear the habit of the *donados* even late in life.[8] This is one of the reasons for the confusion surrounding the question of his profession of vows. The most probable explanation is that Martin, after making his profession, either with permission from his superiors or just out of a kind of stubborn devotion to remaining a servant of the community, continued to wear his beloved *donado* habit until the end of his life. Martin was just that kind of person: stubbornly humble and delightfully free.

## REFLECTION QUESTIONS
Why did Martin become a Dominican brother? How was he able to experience so deeply the unconditional, healing love of God? Do I ever experience being "loved unconditionally"? Do I struggle at times with affirming my own human dignity? What was it about Martin that made him so free? What does it mean for me to be a *brother* or *sister* to others? Read slowly the Canticle of Mary (Lk 1:46–55), praying for the understanding to live what it proclaims.

## NOTES
1. The Order of Friars Preachers, or Dominicans, was founded in the early 1200s by Saint Dominic of Guzmán, to live of life of mendicant poverty and itinerant preaching. The *convento,* or Priory of Our Lady of the Rosary, was composed of about 150 friars at the time Martin entered, not counting the lay brothers and *donados*. JAB, p. 105.
2. ARG, p. 14.
3. Timothy Radcliffe, O.P., Master of the Order of Preachers 1992–2001, "Letters to our Brothers and Sisters in Initial Formation" (May 1999), p. 3.

4. JAB, p. 75.

5. JAB, p. 77. Ruben Vargas Ugarte, S.J., another of Martin's historians, is the one who places this incident in 1596, Martin's second year with the Dominicans (see also JAB, p. 78, note #28).

6. Giuliana Cavallini, *Saint Martin de Porres: Apostle of Charity* (Rockford, Ill.: TAN Books and Publications, 1963), p. 46.

7. There is still some disagreement as to whether Martin ever professed religious vows as a Dominican brother (the *donados* did not profess vows). Busto and Schultz say no, concluding that Martin remained a *donado* all his life (JAB, pp. 77–78), while García-Rivera (AGR, p. 4) and Alvarez defend the tradition and the priory's Book of Professions' entry on the day of Martin's vows. Busto bases his conclusion principally on the use of the phrase *"Hizo **donación** de si"* (He made an **offering** of himself") in the Book's entry for that day. The word *donación* ("offering") comes from the same root word as *donado*. For this reason Busto concludes that Martin's profession on June 2, 1603, was as a *donado*. The use of the word *donación* does not, however, change the fact that Martin professed *vows* on that day. Busto's linguistic argument simply does not stand up to the written record. My own conclusion, after careful consideration of the sources, and after a long conversation with Father Guillermo Alvarez, O.P., a wise Dominican historian in Peru, is that Matin *did*, in fact, make profession as a lay brother. As Father Alvarez notes, the explicit mention of Martin's promising "obedience for his whole life" and his signing of the book as "Brother Marin de Porras" are proof that he made religious profession.

8. JAB, p. 78. In 1615, twelve years after making profession as a lay brother, friar Cipriano de Medina, O.P., comments on seeing Martin, who was "wearing the *donado* habit from his priory, and exercised the duties of infirmarian, barber, and surgeon."

# FOUR

# Martin, Holistic Healer

## FOCUS: SPECIAL GIFTS

Martin de Porres is known for many special gifts, but it as an instrument of God's healing love that he is perhaps best known and revered. We can be quite sure that Martin's tremendous gifts as a healer flowed from his own experience of inner healing. He who had been loved into wholeness by God wanted nothing more than to pass that same healing love of God on to others. Though he had a special concern for the poor, especially Blacks and Indians, Martin's healing knew no borders. Mixing ancient African and indigenous medicinal wisdom with his faith in Jesus Christ, Martin is an example of a true holistic healer, one concerned with the well-being of body, mind, and spirit.

*One day Martin went to visit Father Pedro Montes de Oca, who was in bed because of an illness of the leg. A silly remark made by Martin angered the priest, who then called Martin "a mulatto dog and other bad things." Martin left the cell laughing, and the next day returned with a salad of capers. (Capers are pickled buds of flowers used as ingredients in food preparation.) "Well, father, are you still mad? Eat this little salad of capers which I bring you." The priest was amazed, "for he had wanted such a salad all day being so sick from this illness, suffering from hunger, and also the pain of knowing his leg was to be amputated the following day....Thinking this an act of God, he asked pardon of Brother Martin for the anger and the words." He then asked Martin to take pity on him. Martin laid his hands on the leg, and the friar was healed and freed from danger.*[1]

---

## HEALING WITH GOD'S LOVE

There are hundreds of stories told of Martin healing the sick and the wounded. What makes the preceding story so powerful is that Martin loved and healed even those who treated him with disrespect. His patience and humor with Father Pedro were about much more than just healing a bad leg. Martin wanted to heal the whole person and, in the process, bring healing and reconciliation to the community. A healing in one place brings healing to the whole world.

Martin's gifts of healing began to be nurtured during his early years. In the Malambo neighborhood, he apprenticed under two healers, the first being an *herbalista* or *boticario*, named Mateo Pastor, who taught him the art of preparing herbal medicines. Having learned much about herbs and healing from his mother,[2] Martin was quick to learn the recipes for making creams, salves, and ointments from the abundant flora found on the hills and mountains surrounding Lima. Our Creator God has blessed creation as a source of nutrition and wellness for all living beings. It is only in sharing creation's riches that we show respect to the God who made them.

Martin later spent several years as an apprentice to the barber/

surgeon, Marcelo de Ribera, who became one of Martin's lifetime friends. It was this experience that perhaps best prepared
him for his many years as the assistant infirmarian of the Dominican priory. A *barbero* in Martin's day did just about everything that a family doctor and dentist and pharmacist and nurse
and physical therapist would do today—and a bit more. They cut
hair, pulled teeth, treated burns, dressed and stitched wounds, let
out blood, fixed fractures, did minor surgeries and prescribed
medicines. It was a kind of one-size-fits-all mobile clinic for aches
and pains! For Martin, it was his way of caring for God's people,
being the hands and heart of Christ in the world. For him it was
never a *job* or a *career*; it was a divine calling. Martin knew well
that he was an instrument of God's healing power, and he would
often say to those who were healed, "I cure you; may God heal
you."[3]

Between Martin and the head infirmarian of the *convento*,
Brother Fernando Aragonés, more than two hundred friars and
the hundreds of poor people who flocked to the priory in search
of healing were cared for. Sometimes Martin stayed late into the
night caring for a sick friar or some poor person wounded in a
fight. "He slept wherever the night found him," said one of his
brothers in community, "on a bench, in the Chapter hall, or at
the bedside of one of his patients."[4] The image of Martin faithfully standing watch over the sick late into the night witnesses to
his devotion to Christ, who said, "I was sick and you took care of
me" (Mt 25:36).

For Martin, healing was more than just curing a physical ail-
ment. It was his *presence*, his faithfulness to *being with* the sick,
that communicated God's healing love to them. "He served [the
sick] on his knees, taking care of them throughout the night, one
or two weeks at a time, according to each one's needs. He lifted
them up, helped them lie down, washed them—even those with
the most awful infirmities—his heart aflame like that of an angel."[5]

We see this very same healing presence exemplified in a scene from our own times. Pierre Claverie was a Dominican friar and bishop of the Diocese of Oran—a region in Algeria racked by religious fundamentalism and war. Preaching in June 1996, the bishop spoke of his own desire to be faithful to his Christian vocation in a country so sickened by violence, and what it means to "stand watch" alongside the poor and the vulnerable:

> People have often asked me: "What do you do there? Why do you stay?...Go back home!" Home....Where is our home?...We are there [in Algeria] because of this crucified Messiah. Because of nothing else and no one else!...We are there like someone at the bedside of a friend, or of a sick brother, in silence, holding his hand, and wiping his brow. Because of Jesus, because it is he who suffers there, in this violence that spares no one, crucified anew in the flesh of thousands of innocent people."[6]

"We are there because of Jesus." This is what it means to be *present* to those who suffer. This is the healing love that Martin so beautifully expressed with his life. Five weeks after preaching this homily, on August 1, 1996, Bishop Claverie was assassinated in front of his home in Oran. Like Martin, he had kept vigil through the long, dark night—*there*—alongside his people.

Martin, too, was faithful—always there—for the poor and the sick. One day they brought him an African slave, who had been wounded in a fight, his entrails hanging out. Martin immediately ran up to his cell and brought down some wine and rosemary. "He *knelt down* next to the black man and began to suck the blood from the gaping wound. He then washed it with the wine and dressed the wound with rosemary which he chewed into a paste." Four days later the man was well.[7] We certainly are not accustomed to such vivid images—someone sucking blood from a wound—but we must not fail to see what lies hidden in it: Martin *kneeling* at the side of a bloodied body, *kissing* the wounds, healing them with the same wine that is used in the celebration of the Eucharist. As Bishop Claverie said, "It is Jesus who suffers there...crucified anew in the flesh of thousands of innocent people."

Martin often used herbs and natural remedies in his healings, many of which he grew himself in the priory garden. Like Jesus, who used mud, saliva, and water, Martin used paste from ground almond and melon seeds, alfalfa, chamomile, and rosemary, even hot bricks which he placed over cramps. He was *curandero*[8] and saint all in one. This was the way he communicated the unconditional love and consoling presence of God to others.

Today we might imagine Martin supporting many of the alternative paths of healing that have their roots in ancient wisdom: naturopathic and herbal medicine, acupuncture and Reiki, massage and reflexology, twelve-step groups, meditation, and hospice care. Martin, like Jesus, frequently healed through touch. Are we aware of the power and reverence of human touch? Does it not remind us that we have been fashioned by the hand of a loving God?

Mary Ellen is a modern-day healer. Each year, on Holy Thursday, she and her companions give massages through healing touch to street people in a poor neighborhood in San Francisco. Like Jesus, who washed the feet of his disciples on that day, Mary Ellen pours her love out through the power of human touch to give back to the abused and battered poor their very own human dignity. She, like Martin, preaches the Good News through her hands.

## REFLECTION QUESTIONS

What is the healing that I most desire? Have I considered asking Saint Martin to intercede for me? When I ask God to heal others, am I willing to be God's instrument? How can I make use of the natural and holistic avenues for healing? Read the story of the ten lepers healed by Jesus (Lk 17:11–19). Is there a healing in my life for which I want to give thanks to God? Have I ever considered myself a healer? How can I give to others the healing love that flows from the heart and hands of Christ?

## NOTES

1. ARG, p. 72.
2. ARG, p. 3.
3. JAB, pp. 122, 270.
4. JAB, p. 96. Testimonies from Francisco de Arce, O.P., and Marcelo de Ribera.
5. JAB, p. 123. Testimony of Brother Cristóbal de San Juan.
6. Bishop Pierre Claverie preached this homily on June 23, 1996, at the Dominican Monastery of Our Lady of Prouille, in southern France, five weeks before his assassination. A book in French by Father Jean Jacques Pérennès, O.P., has been published in his memory.
7. JAB, p. 109.
8. A *curandero*, from the verb *curar*, "to cure," is a shamanlike healer who uses a mixture of herbal medicine, prayer, and, at times, a bit of superstition in his or her healing practice. Many ancient tribes and cultures continue to have recourse to this kind of healing today.

## FIVE

# God Calls Forth a Prophet

### FOCUS: BELL RINGER OF LIMA

Besides his duties as assistant infirmarian, another of Martin's conventual chores was to ring the church bells. He was famous throughout the city of Lima as the *campanero*[1] of the Dominican priory. In fact, whenever the neighbors, for one reason or another, failed to hear the early morning bells ring, they immediately concluded that Brother Martin had fallen ill.[2] What is interesting is that, in the testimonies collected for Martin's beatification, many of his contemporaries shared stories about Martin's devotion to ringing the *campana del alba*, the early morning bell, rung at about 4:30 A.M.—just before the first rays of the sun pierced the dark sky. Why such a devotion to ringing bells? What word was God speaking to Martin's contemplative heart during those early morning hours?

*A master carpenter from Spain, Francisco Pérez Quintero, told this story about Martin's duties as the priory "campanero": "Every night a large white, black, and brown cat would come through a vent that opened into [Martin's] cell....When he had reached him, the cat would begin to pull on his habit with its paws as if he were giving him signs that it was time for some duty....Brother Martin de Porras would leave the cell to ring the dawn bell ('campana del alba') to which he was devoted....The cat following in his tracks."*[3]

## A MESTIZO CAT

This story is a cat lover's delight! Thanks to the groundbreaking work on the "little stories" of Martin de Porres by theologian Alex García-Rivera, we know that this story is much more than just a cute anecdote about a cat. Says García-Rivera:

> Given the...violent encounter of Iberian, sub-Saharan African, and Amerindian cultures, the appearance of the white, black, and brown cat is striking....This *mestizo* cat, after all, wakes up the other *mestizo*, the mulatto Martin, and "reminds" him of his duty....By ringing the dawn bell, Saint Martin...is responsible for waking up the Church from her sleep to begin a new day. This white, black, and brown cat signifies something to do with the bell, usually a harbinger of important news or, more significantly, the transmitter of an important message.[4]

It is through the telling of this seemingly innocent story about Martin's feline friend that we glimpse the profound meaning of Martin's *devotion* to ringing the dawn bells each day. Martin, who carried deep within his heart a vision of the reign of God, knew that the Church had not yet *awakened* to its proper role as the leaven of a new society. He *saw* the contradictions, the racist laws, the unjust conquest of America by "Catholic" Spain, and he was painfully aware of the Church's deafening silence on these matters. The Church was asleep while bandits ransacked an entire continent.

So Martin and his mestizo cat teamed up as co-conspirators in an attempt to wake up the Dominican Order and the Church to a deeper understanding of God's justice. Martin, like the prophet Isaiah, heard a voice deep within his heart, asking, "Whom shall I send?" (Isa 6:8). Who will speak God's Word of justice, equality, and love in the midst of this violence? Who will have the courage to proclaim the words of the ancient prophets in a new language for our day? "Here am I, Lord," prayed Martin, "send me" (Isa 6:8).

Less than one hundred years before Martin began ringing the bells of the priory in Lima, another community of Dominican friars, on the island of Hispaniola (Dominican Republic) in the Caribbean, was sounding its own wake-up call. Not long after arriving on the island, the friars began to see the contradictions and the lies behind the European conquest of the Americas. One of their own, Antonio de Montesinos, was called forth to sound the cry for justice:

> I am the voice of Christ crying out in the desert of this island…the most shocking and dangerous voice you have ever heard….With what right and by which justice do you hold these Indians in such horrible servitude? By what authority do you carry out such detestable wars against the people of these lands—people so meek and peaceful? Are these not human beings?…Are you not obliged to love them as yourselves?[5]

Martin, taking his place in a long line of prophets, knew that *somebody* had to ring the bells to wake this generation up from its lethargic sleep. Someone had to show that it is possible to live harmoniously and peacefully in a world that is *white, black, and brown* all at the same time. So each morning, Martin and his clandestine calico cat did their part to usher in the dawn of a new day. The bells were rung as the friars sang the morning office of *lauds*, just about the time in which Zechariah's Canticle (Lk 1:78–79) announced the dawning of a new day:

> By the tender mercy of our God, the dawn from on high will break upon us, to give light to those who sit in darkness and in the shadow of death, to guide our feet into the way of peace.

It was Martin's duty to help the "dawn from on high" break into the darkness of imperialism and its sinister shadow of death. Martin knew that God, who hears the cry of the poor, would faithfully guide the Church "into the way of peace."

Is it a simple coincidence of history or might it be God's mysterious plan that three and a half centuries after Martin de Porres started ringing the bells of the Dominican priory in Lima, God raised up *another prophet named Martin* who shared the vision of a society in which white, black, and brown people might live together? Was the tricolored calico cat not a divine sign from God, one that continues to manifest itself today in new ways?

On August 28, 1963, *the other Martin*, Martin Luther King, Jr., spoke the following words in front of the Lincoln Memorial in Washington, D.C.

> We have come to this hallowed spot to remind America of the fierce urgency of now....Now is the time to rise from the dark and desolate valley of segregation to the sunlit path of racial justice....I have a dream that one day this nation will rise up and live out the true meaning of its creed....I have a dream that my four children will one day live in a nation where they will not be judged by the color of their skin, but by the content of their character....I have a dream...that one day...little black boys and black

girls will be able to join hands with little white boys and girls as sisters and brothers....[And] when we let freedom ring, when we let it ring from every village and every hamlet, from every state and every city....[we] will be able to join hands and sing in the words of the old Negro spiritual, "Free at last! Free at last! Thank God Almighty, we are free at last."[6]

It is quite likely that Martin de Porres and his multicolored cat were present in the vast crowd gathered in Washington, D.C., that day, smiling upon the *other* Martin, as the bells of freedom rang out loud and clear. After all, just the previous year Martin de Porres had been declared a saint of the Church.

Some have speculated that it was the unaddressed racism within the Church that postponed Martin's canonization for almost three hundred years. There is probably some truth to the speculation. At the same time, though, it just may be that God has the final word in the unfolding of history. Is it not of tremendous value that Pope John XXIII had the prophetic courage to declare Martin a saint right in the midst of both the Second Vatican Council and the civil rights movement in the United States? Is there not good reason to suspect that Martin de Porres was intimately involved in these historical events? One cannot help but hear in the voices of both Martins the ancient cry of the prophets, announcing the dawning of a new day of justice.[7]

## REFLECTION QUESTIONS

What bells need to be rung today to *wake up our Church* as both Martins did in their day? Go back and read the Canticle of Zechariah (Lk 1:68–79), praying over this ancient hymn which is sung throughout the world as the sun rises each day. Write in a journal or notebook your prayerful reflections. If Martin's cat were to appear today where I live, what colors would it be? What languages would it speak? Spend some time praying for tolerance and an end to racial, political and religious injustice in the world.

## NOTES

1. The companero was in charge of ringing the bell, *campana,* which called the friars to prayer throughout the day and night. The city's convent and church bells also served as public clocks.
2. JAB, pp. 82–85.
3. AGR, p. 59, and JAB, p. 83.
4. AGR, p. 59.
5. This very famous homily, preached by friar Antonio de Montesinos, O.P., on the Fourth Sunday of Advent, 1511, was recorded by a young diocesan priest who was present that day in the church. His name was Bartolomé de las Casas, and he became the most forceful prophet for justice and defense of the rights of the Amerindians during the colonial years. Cited from Bartolomé de las Casas, *History of the Indies,* translated and edited by Andrée Collard (New York: Harper & Row, 1971), III, pp. 182–184.
6. Dr. Martin Luther King, Jr., "I Have A Dream," given in Washington, D.C., on August 28, 1963; cited in *Ebony* (January 1986), pp. 40–42.
7. Martin Luther King, Jr., was assassinated in Memphis, Tennessee, in 1968. Today, connected to the Church of St. Peter in Memphis, is the Saint Martin de Porres Shrine, under the direction of the Dominican Province of Saint Martin de Porres. Besides being a place of prayer and pilgrimage, the shrine is also dedicated to furthering the work of social and racial justice in the spirit of *both* Martins. The address of the shrine is P.O. Box 3111, Memphis, TN 38173.

## SIX

# A New Heaven and a New Earth

## FOCUS: TRAGEDY AVERTED

"God's ways are not our ways"—a truth that is still difficult at times for us to accept. And so we find ourselves looking back and wondering why God allows certain things to happen. Most of us know some tragic story about a person being in the wrong place at the wrong time—a car accident that shouldn't have happened, a divorce that could have been avoided, the death of a loved one that makes no sense whatsoever. When one looks back at the chaos and destruction caused by the conquest of America and the trafficking of millions of African slaves, one is tempted to wonder if maybe God just fell asleep that day. Would it not have been better if Europe, America, and Africa had simply never met? It is like wondering what our world would be like if the atomic bomb had not been invented or if Jesus had not been crucified. If Martin is the fruit of a tragic "mistake" in history, then what does he teach us about God?

*María Beltrán was the daughter of an important military officer in Lima. In the midst of her difficult labor, and unable to give birth to the child (la criatura) who was stuck in the birth canal, the relics of different saints were placed on her belly with the hope of obtaining some divine help. Nothing happened, and she was advised to make her confession and prepare for death. At that moment Lupercia González de Mendoza, the mother of María, "remembered she had a piece of the sleeve from the habit of the venerable servant of God, Brother Martin de Porras," and she took it and placed it over the witness' belly and asked fervently [of Saint Martin] to intercede with his divine Majesty to give a good birth. At that very moment the child was born healthily, "without being crippled or with any other wound."*[1]

## NEW BIRTH

Again we turn to the insights of Alex García-Rivera for our starting point. With a keen eye for reading these stories, he notes that "the first clue that this is not going to be like other miraculous stories is that relics of Old World saints are placed on Doña María's belly without any effect....It is the relic of a would-be New World saint, a saint that is yet-to-be, that has effect."[2] This story is about something *new* that is happening, or about to happen—a new kind of holiness, a new kind of Church that is being born. And Martin de Porres is part of this wonderful, new birth that God is bringing about in a land conquered and devastated by war and destruction.

We are being invited, through a story like this, to set aside our previous convictions and ways of thinking, and open ourselves to new possibilities. This is what conversion is about—turning around and seeing life from a new perspective. Before we continue, though, it is important to make one very clear statement: God never wills evil or injustice. The conquest of the Americas by Spain was both. But having said that, we must also be challenged to see with the eyes of faith, that is, see what marvels

God does in the wake of our human mistakes and blunders. God did not *will* the violent death of Jesus, but through his resurrection from the dead, we can testify to the fact that God works marvels: *"O! Felix culpa!!"* O! Happy fault!"[3]

Martin de Porres is a living example of God's marvelous actions in the midst of our sinful and broken world. Martin was a "mistake." His mother's people should never have been captured and shipped to a foreign land against their will. His Spanish father had no right to be part of an occupying army in the sacred land of the Incas, and he certainly was wrong in fathering a child and then practically abandoning him and his mother. God's ways, though, are not our ways. God has a way of fashioning something new from the broken pieces of our mistakes.

Martin is a symbol of this *something new* which God is creating. The coming together of his African soul and his *latino* warrior's heart—itself the fruit of an unjust mistake of history—is a living example of how God is creating "a new heaven and a new earth" (Rev 21:1). As the story of the birth of María Beltrán's child shows, Martin is a *new world* saint in an *old world*. He shatters the old molds, because he is part of a new creation. He is a *mestizo*, a mixture of ancestral bloodlines and cultures and histories and dreams. He is a mixture of wars and violence and rape and conquest. He is all of this.[4] And he is God's beloved child—dark brown clay in the hands of the divine Potter: "See, I am making all things new" (Rev 21:5).

> A great portent appeared in heaven: a woman clothed with the sun, with the moon under her feet, and on her head a crown of twelve stars. She was pregnant and was crying out in birth pangs, in the agony of giving birth.... Then [a] dragon stood before the woman who was about to bear a child, so that he might devour her child as soon as it was born. And she gave birth to a son, a male child, who is to rule all the nations.
>
> *Revelation 12:1–5*

The story of María Beltrán's difficult birth, aided by the prayer-ful intercession of Martin de Porres, is a kind of retelling of this story from the Book of Revelation. It is a story about God birthing new life in the face of death. It is the story of Martin's birth and his place in the new *mestizo* society. The *old world* relics no longer work. The *old* ways have come and gone. The *old* structures of power and domination, of conquest and slavery, are now giving way to the *new heaven and the new earth*. History's "mistake" is redeemed by the God of history.

This is equally true with the "mistake" called Martin de Porres, "son of an unknown father and a freed slave woman." His very life of contradiction becomes a wide-open space for God to fash-ion *a new creation in Christ* (see 2 Cor 5:17). Martin is the Peru-vian version of Mexico's María de Guadalupe. In the same way that she, the dark-skinned and pregnant Virgin of Guadalupe, gave birth to a *mestizo* society and Church, so too with Martin. His dark skin—the product of one of history's tragic "mistakes"— is transformed into a Word-Made-Flesh which announces the birth of a new People of God.

The European Church that arrived on the shores of indig-enous America, ancient Africa, and mysterious Asia "has been groaning in labor pains" for two thousand long years (Rom 8:22). Finally, even despite strong opposition in every age, the Church is beginning to take on a new face. It is becoming *every* color, *every* language, *every* people, *every* way of life. At last the secret of Pentecost is beginning to seep into the cracks of the Church's walls, and we are again hearing the marvels of God proclaimed in every language under heaven (Acts 2:1–13).

Life is full of mistakes. We all look back and wonder what would life have been like without the wars and the bombs, the gas chambers and the thoughtless bursts of anger that severed sacred ties. What would our story be like if Christ had not been crucified by hatred? We cannot know, for the road of history took other turns. But what we *do* know, and what Martin de Porres teaches us time and time again, is that God is not yet finished creating the universe. We are the clay in the hands of the Potter, and nothing is impossible with God.

## REFLECTION QUESTIONS

Am I willing to trust that the mistakes and blunders of my life can be re-created through God's infinite love? Do I trust God's providence, even when it seems so unfathomable? Does my faith community reflect the *new* people of God, rich in diversity? Evil and injustice are as real in our world today as in Martin's day. How can I offer my life as a *wide open space* for God to fashion a *new creation in Christ*? Pray and reflect on Psalm 139.

## NOTES

1. AGR, p. 88. The testimony was given by María Beltrán herself.
2. AGR, pp. 88–89.
3. "Oh! Happy fault...which gained for us so great a Redeemer." *Felix Culpa* is an ancient phrase, sung each year in the *Exultet* at the Easter Vigil service. It is a reference to the blessed fruits of the resurrection, flowing from the terrible crime of the cross. For more on this, see Alejandro R. García-Rivera, *A Wounded Innocence: Sketches for a Theology of Art* (Collegeville, Minn.: The Liturgical Press), 2003, pp. 92–93
4. García-Rivera highlights the very important work of Virgilio Elizondo, the principle architect of the emerging *mestizo theology*. See AGRs bibliography for sources.

# SEVEN

# God's Creatures

## FOCUS: LOVE FOR ALL

Everyone knows Saint Francis of Assisi and his love songs to brother sun and sister moon. In our days of growing ecological consciousness (in response to the constant assault on the earth and her resources), we need the symbol of Saint Francis to encourage us in the struggle. Martin had his own way of loving creation and celebrating God as Creator. As a friar of the Order of Preachers, Martin's friendship with animals and all of God's creatures was not just a hobby. It was a kind of catechesis for Martin, a holy preaching that always pointed to God and the all-inclusiveness of God's kingdom of love. In the end, the stories about Martin's affection for God's creatures are really stories *about* us and *for* us. They are the gospel, the good news according to Martin.

*Martin's friend, the barber/surgeon Marcelo de Ribera, recalls the time that some bulls and calves were brought to the priory so that the professed brothers could play with them during their recreation. Martin heard, though, that the animals had been without food or water for four days, and this pained him deeply. Martin quickly began to collect barrels of water and hay that he brought over from the priory stables. After midnight, when all the friars were asleep, Martin distributed the water and hay to the hungry animals, each according to its age. The wild animals became tame, and some, it is said, came to Martin and kissed his habit. One friar, Diego de la Fuente, was standing at his window and overheard Martin say to the bulls, "Now, brother, you are older, let the younger ones eat."[1]*

## CHRIST EVERYWHERE AND ALWAYS

"Let the younger ones eat." We glimpse here not only Martin's tender affection for God's creatures, but we hear him preaching on the need to be attentive to the youngest and the least among us, as well. The story is similar to Jesus' parable of the sheep and the goats and the coming of the reign of God: "Just as you did it to one of the least of these who are members of my family, you did it to me" (Mt 25:40). When Martin tells the bulls not to forget the little ones, we, who hear the story many centuries later, are privileged to overhear the conversation and the gospel message it proclaims.

It is important, then, for us to hear these stories not as if we were looking at a family album and seeing photographs of "darling little Martin," surrounded by animals at the local petting zoo. Martin's animals are the world. He loved them because he loved the world and all that God had made. When Martin spoke to his furry friends, he was speaking from the depths of his heart and soul. It was his preaching, a preaching intended for his Dominican brothers and for us. Every word from Martin's mouth must be heard in this way. He was, after all, a friar preacher; his whole being was saturated with the gospel of Christ.

This is not to say that Martin did not have fun "horsing around" with his animal friends, and that it was all serious business. Not at all! He genuinely loved them, and that is why they were the means he used to preach the gospel. Once, while Martin was frolicking with a bunch of calves on a farm outside of Lima, his friend Juan Vásquez de Parra said, "Father, be careful that they don't knock you down." Martin responded, "Don't worry. I promise you that I haven't had a better day in all my life!"[2] Martin's love for animals was genuine, because his *love* was genuine.

Martin was perhaps best known for his love of dogs. They would cuddle up to him and lavishly lick him to express their affection. One witness said that he frequently saw Martin returning to the priory "bringing with him wounded or sick dogs. He would cure them with great attentiveness and love, almost as if they were rational beings."[3] What was he trying to say to the world by bringing these dogs into the priory to heal them? What was he saying about God? Dominican sister Mary O'Driscoll asked during a conference almost twenty years ago: "Do the poor feel comfortable in our homes?" Is that not the question Martin wants us to ask ourselves? Do the poor feel comfortable in our country? Martin's stray and wounded dogs certainly felt very comfortable in Martin's simple cell. They were his little brothers and his sisters.

Not everyone, though, saw the situation through Martin's eyes. At one point the Dominican provincial ordered Martin to throw all the dogs out of the cloister. One witness testified that Martin, "moved with pity and compassion, gathered as many dogs as he could," and took them to the house of his sister, Juana. Each morning he arrived with food hidden in the folds of his habit to feed them. Needless to say, Juana's generosity also reached its limit. She complained that the dogs were turning the house into a mess, so Martin called them together, "and speaking with the dogs, told them that when they had to do their *necessities*, to go out into the street....After that the dogs no longer bothered anyone."[4] Hospitality towards the homeless is not always neat and clean. Still though, we hear the voice say, "I was a stranger and you welcomed me" (Mt 25:35).

Martin was also in charge of the clothing room of the priory, and even *his* patience was tested when he realized that the mice were destroying the bedding and gowns used for the sick. He finally caught one of the mice and said, "Brother, why are you and your friends damaging the linens for the sick? I'm not going to kill you, but go and call your companions, and together go out to the garden. I will bring you food each day." So daily Martin took the leftovers from the infirmary out to feed the mice."[5] "I was hungry and you gave me food" (Mt 25:35).

There are hundreds of stories like these. They offer us an insight into Martin's vision of a world where the "least of my brothers and sisters" would be cared for through simple gestures of charity. He lived this out until the very end of his life. As he was dying, the friars tried to give him medicines made from animals that were killed. Martin gathered up enough strength to speak one more word in defense of *the least of these*. "Why do you kill those *creatures of God* if it is God's will for me to die?"[6]

Through the stories of Martin's compassion for God's creatures, he is urging us to "wake up" and realize that there are *little ones* among us, too. They are here in our very midst—hungry and thirsty, wounded and abandoned. Sometimes they are calves or dogs, but more often they are children or refugees fleeing war or women hiding in a battered women's shelter. The word for "creature" in Spanish—*criatura*—refers not only to animals (a mule, a mosquito, a mouse), but is also used when referring to an infant, a newborn baby, a "little one." For Martin *all* God's little ones are *criaturas de Dios* ("creatures of God").[7] When Martin embraces a wounded dog, he is embracing every *human* who has been wounded as well. And, as Martin and the gospel remind us, each compassionate embrace is always an embrace of Christ: "Whatever you did for one of the least of these brothers or sisters of mine, you did for me."

This spontaneous love affair with all of God's creatures is the homily of Martin's life, his preaching of the gospel of Christ. Without an abundance of words, Martin's actions proclaim the reign of God in a thunderous voice. Jesus said, "Blessed are the eyes that see what you see! For I tell you that many prophets and kings desired to see what see, but did not see it, and to hear what you hear, but did not hear it" (Lk 10:23–24). The question for us is: Do we *see* what Martin is doing and *hear* what he is saying? Do we *see* the little ones in our midst? Do we *hear* the cry of the poor? And most importantly, do we see and hear that *they* are Christ?

## REFLECTION QUESTIONS

What does Martin's affection and love for animals say to me? Do I *get* what Martin is doing through his "preaching of the little ones"? How does Martin's example challenge me to discover Christ in "the least of my brothers and sisters"? How can I make of my life a lived homily about God's love for the poor? Read Matthew 25:31–46. Where am I in this parable? Where is our country? Spend some time with an animal, a pet, showing it affection and love. Then close your eyes and send this loving kindness out to our wounded world.

## NOTES

1. JAB, p. 202. Martin's friend, Marcelo de Ribera, gave this testimony.
2. JAB, p. 289. Juan Vásquez de Parra told this story.
3. JAB, p. 289. Joseph Pizarro, from Cusco, gave this testimony.
4. JAB, p. 292. This story was told by Cataline de Porras: Juana's daughter, Martin's niece.
5. JAB, p. 293. Another testimony given by Marcelo de Ribera.
6. JAB, p. 294. This story was told by Juan Vásquez de Parra, Martin's close friend.

7. García-Rivera does a fine job looking at the many levels of meaning surrounding the word *criatura* in the little stories. See AGR, ch. 7, pp. 85–105.

## EIGHT

# The Garden of God

### FOCUS: LOVE FOR ALL CREATION

Every living being was, for Martin, a manifestation of the grandeur and beauty of God. If the animals were his friends, then the earth, with its many trees and plants, was his playground. Martin loved the fecundity of the earth, its fertility and plentifulness. It all spoke to him of the gratuitousness of God. The cloister gardens at both Santo Domingo priory and the neighboring Priory of La Recoleta were places where Martin could be alone and creative, witnessing the miracles of nature and God's goodness.[1] The many medicinal plants which Martin grew in the gardens were all part of his own clandestine, nongovernmental drug-prescription program: God's free medicine for the poor!

*"The LORD God planted a garden in Eden, in the east; and there [God] put the [human] whom he had formed [from the dust of the ground]. Out of the ground the LORD God made to grow every*

45

*tree that is pleasant to the sight and good for food, the tree of life also in the midst of the garden, and the tree of the knowledge of good and evil. A river flows out of Eden to water the garden"* (Gen 2:8–10).

*"Then the angel showed me the river of the water of life…flowing from the throne of God and of the Lamb through the middle of the street of the city. On either side of the river is the tree of life with its twelve kinds of fruit, producing its fruit each month; and the leaves of the tree are for the healing of the nations"* (Rev 22:1–2).

---

## SYMBOL OF LIFE AND DEATH

The two quotes above stand like bookends on either end of the Judeo-Christian scriptures. Our story of salvation begins and ends in a garden teeming with life. In the Gospel of John, Jesus is crucified and rises from the dead in a garden (19:41; 20:15). The garden is the symbol of life and death and life again. "Unless a grain of wheat falls into the earth and dies, it remains just a single grain; but if it dies, it bears much fruit" (Jn 12:24). Martin felt right at home in God's garden.

Every year, during the month of July, Martin and his friend Juan,[2] hiked up into the hills north of Lima, to an area called Los Amancaes.[3] They always went following the celebrations commemorating the Feast of Saint John the Baptist.[4] For Martin it was a chance to get away for some much-needed solitude and see the last of the golden *amancaes*. It was up in the hills that Martin communed with the earth and all her beauty. Like Saint Francis, Martin was in love with creation, but in a way similar to his passion for the animals, Martin's love for the earth was deeply connected with his love for the poor.

On one of the treks up into the hills of Amancaes, Martin instructed Juan to join him in sowing *manzanilla* (chamomile) seeds in the hoof prints that the cattle had left in the wet ground.

Juan commented that it seemed rather futile to sow seeds there, as the cattle would simply eat the plants once they began to grow. According to Juan, Martin began laughing, and responded that this would be a good way of pruning the plants so that they would grow even stronger. Juan again tried to dissuade Martin, but this time Martin told his friend that it was his job to return every few days to check on the plants and to keep the cattle away. Says Juan in his testimony, "Three days later I went back to that place and found it surrounded by cattle. The plants were thriving—as if they had been growing there for more than a year."[5]

On another occasion, while they were walking in the same hills, Martin cut off a branch of a fig tree and carried it to the top of the hill, where he dug a hole and planted it. Two weeks later he and Juan returned to the spot. "Father," remarked Juan, "the fig tree you planted eighteen days ago is already budding," to which Martin responded, "Thanks be to God, within two or three years it will bear fruit for the poor who pass by this way."[6] For Martin, the earth was God's garden of plenty. It belonged to everyone—even the cattle, but especially to the poor.

Martin's love for creation has much to teach us in an age in which we live stressed with work, making money, being successful. In this frenzied rhythm of life, we so easily lose sight of the fact that God is providing for our needs, caring for us with a gardener's love. So what if the cows eat the *manzanilla*, Martin said with his lighthearted humor, we will have healthier cows *and* stronger plants!

> "Do not worry about your life," [says Jesus]...."Look at the birds of the air; they neither sow nor reap nor gather into barns, and yet your heavenly Father feeds them.... Consider the lilies of the field, how they grow; they neither toil nor spin, yet I tell you, even Solomon in all his glory was not clothed like one of these....Strive first for the kingdom of God and his righteousness, and all these things will be given to you as well."
>
> *Matthew 6:25–33*

Martin worked hard, but he knew that he was not in control of the fruits of his labor. That was up to the Lord of the harvest. As the psalmist says, "The earth is the LORD's and all that is in it, / the world and those who live in it" (Ps 24:1). Because of this deep trust in Divine Providence, Martin never abused God's creation to further his own greed or power. There was no need to fence in his own private property, leaving the cattle excluded from the garden of God's goodness. How different our times have become! Nations battle to protect their borders, building fences and walls of self-enslavement. Wars are being waged to control the world's oil reserves. Why so much greed? Where is our trust in God and in one another? Have we lost sight of the gratuitousness of life?

A few years ago a Dominican friar was visiting a community of Mayan Indians in the northern part of Guatemala. The land in this area was lush and green, covered with fields of corn and beans. Surrounding the huts in the village were mango, papaya, banana, and orange trees, not to mention the colorful flowers growing everywhere. The friar, who had been a worker priest in Spain and was familiar with different experiments in cooperative farming, was impressed not only with the beauty of the land, but also with what appeared to be a high level of production. In a conversation with one of the village leaders later in the day, the friar asked, "Is the land here in your village divided up and owned privately or do you own it communally through a cooperative?" He was hoping that the farmer would affirm that the latter was the case. The indigenous peasant looked at the friar with a confused look on his face, and after a rather long pause, replied, "Own the land? How can someone own his own mother?"[7]

"Blessed are the meek," [said Jesus,] "for they will inherit the earth" (Mt 5:5).

We have become accustomed to a way of life that is far from the design of our Creator. Millions of acres of Brazilian rain forests have been sold and cut down—as if we were dealing with onions or tomatoes in a market. Agribusinesses and megalandowners have run the poor and middle classes off of the land. Factories pollute our waterways, depleted uranium is used to fight our wars, and asthmatic children are suffocating in our cities.

The hills surrounding Lima today are barren deserts. Not a blade of grass can be seen for miles. There are no more yellow *amancaes* to signal the coming of the feast of Saint John the Baptist. And as the flowers wither and the fields dry up, so do the poor. When Martin planted his fig tree on the top of the hill, he did so thinking of coming generations: "Thanks be to God, within two or three years it will bear fruit for the poor who pass by this way."

The poor continue to pass by that very spot, but the fig tree is gone. We need more Martins who are courageous enough to fall in love with the earth again.


## REFLECTION QUESTIONS

Am I aware of the daily destruction and sale of the earth by the forces of greed in our world? What can I do to protect God's creation? Looking back at Martin's life, how did he connect his love of the earth with his love for the poor? Am I aware of how pharmaceutical companies have led us into forgetting the medicinal herbs and the natural remedies of our grandparents? Am I willing to reclaim that ancient wisdom? Read a few lines from Psalm 104 each day this week, reflecting on their significance in our world today. Sow a garden or pot a plant and tend it as a reminder of God's gratuitous love for us.


## NOTES

1. Along with the cloister garden of his own priory, Martin also spent time tending the plants and praying in the garden at the Dominican Priory of La Recoleta. This was where his good

friend, Brother Juan Macías, lived. When Martin was not in one of the gardens, he could usually be found in the infirmary, the belfry, or the *portería*. The *portería* was the door that opened to the street, and this was where Martin cared for the needs of the poor who came to the priory begging for food, medicine, healing, and someone to listen to their problems.

2. On most of Martin's adventures outside of the priory, he was accompanied by his faithful friend, Juan Vásquez de Parra. See chapter 12 for more biographical information on Juan.

3. The *amancae* is a yellow flower that, in Martin's day, blanketed the hills surrounding Lima, reaching its peak during the month of June with the feast of Saint John the Baptist (June 24). This was a festival that the whole city participated in, but is remembered in history particularly for the music, dancing, and animated celebration of the African slaves, mulattos, and zambos (the offspring between a black and an Indian, though it could also refer to a person from China (see also JAB, p. 32). Most of the servants and slaves were present during the Amancaes festivities, accompanying their masters and *patrones*, or bosses. While the "official" festivities were being celebrated, the Africans and African descendants had their own parallel (and apparently quite lively) festivities. JAB, p. 299.

4. The Peruvian province of Dominicans is under the patronage of Saint John the Baptist, so the annual feast day was filled with solemn celebrations at the priory. Juan, Martin's friend, is the one who recalls these yearly excursions into the hills. JAB, p. 299.

5. JAB, p. 300.

6. JAB, p. 300.

7. This story was told to the author in 1992 by a Dominican friar working in Guatemala.

## NINE

# Prayer: The Foundation

### FOCUS: ALONE WITH GOD

When all is said and done, it was prayer that formed the foundation upon which Martin's entire life was built. It was prayer that transformed Martin from the "son of an unknown father" to beloved child of God. A friend of mine, Brother Herman de Porres, who, as a Dominican and an African-American, has modeled his life on Martin's, says this about the saint from Peru, "We know that he was a true brother to everyone he encountered. One could say a lot regarding his relations with neighbors; however it was his relation with God that makes him a significant figure worthy of imitation. Every moment of Martin's life was the result of his intimate relations with the Master...a real and loving God."[1]

*"After receiving communion [Martin] would withdraw in silence to pray to God, so much so that even when they [the friars] would look for him, they could not find him....Sometimes he would hide*

*beneath one of the chairs in the Chapter hall of the priory, or in a loft or basement....One day some of the friars were looking for Martin all over the priory. Not finding him, they knocked on the door of Francisco de la Torre, a guest of the priory, who offered to help look for Martin. He found him hidden in a solitary corner up on the roof of the church, on his knees praying, his hands folded with great devotion, looking toward the place where the Blessed Sacrament was kept in the church."[2]*

## LOST IN THE COMPANY OF GOD

Prayer was Martin's daily bread. It was what nourished him. From childhood he had shown a great inclination towards silence and solitude. One of Martin's Dominican ancestors, the medieval mystic and theologian, Meister Eckhart, said once that "the very best and noblest attainment in this life is to be silent and let God work and speak within." And again, Eckhart added, "If Jesus is to speak in the soul, she must be all alone, and she has to be quiet."[3]

Martin knew this need for silence and aloneness with God almost by instinct. It was a gift given him by God, though not everyone understood it. It was uncommon in Martin's time for the *donados* and lay brothers to attend Mass and receive Communion every day. That meant that *Communion days* were special days—Sundays and solemn feasts. Martin celebrated these special feasts by spending the day hiding out in silent prayer with God. After receiving the Eucharist with his brothers at the conventual Mass, it only seemed natural to Martin to go and put into practice the words of the psalmist: "O taste and see that the LORD is good" (34:8).

In the Dominican tradition, of which Martin was a part, all activity, including preaching and works of charity, were meant to flow from contemplation. The Order's motto, *Contemplari et contemplata aliis tradere,* translates as "Contemplate and share with others that which is contemplated." Martin's intense apostolic activity and compassionate service to the poor was intensely rooted in a life of prayer and contemplation. Without one, it is rare to see the other. Another great Dominican, Catherine of Siena, wrote to a friend of the need to be faithful to both contemplation *and* loving service, "You must walk, not with one, but two feet."[4] In her own prayer, God had said to her, "Love of me and love of neighbor are one and the same thing."[5]

Understanding Martin's intense life of prayer as *one* of the two feet on which he walked helps us to translate his saintly life into a workable and healthy spiritual life for ourselves. It is not that Martin *ran away* from the friars or from the poor so that he could hide out and pray. Running away from the world does not make one into a contemplative. As God told Catherine of Siena, "Love of me and love of neighbor are one and the same thing."

For Martin, to receive the body of Christ in the Eucharist only seemed complete if he could then go off and be alone, in order to love God *and* the poor in the silence of his heart. It was the very same poor with whom he would break bread later in the day. His silence and solitude was intimate communion with God *and* with the world. The bread he shared with the poor was simply a continuation of the eucharistic celebration. In Martin's silent prayer these two dimensions—which often are separate— came together.

We too frequently experience a separation between the liturgical practice of our faith and our commitment to justice. Bartolomé de las Casas, OP, who had forcefully denounced the conquest and slaughter of the Indians and Africans in America, said once, speaking of the link between the Eucharist and the poor, "They cannot celebrate the Eucharist with bread that has been kneaded by the hands of enslaved brothers and sisters." And to a bishop who did nothing to link his faith with justice, Las Casas added, "You eat and drink the blood of your own flock."[6] Saint Paul also made clear the connection between the Eucharist and the people of God:

The bread that we break, is it not a sharing in the body of Christ? Because there is one bread, we who are many are one body, for we all partake of the one bread (1 Cor 10:16–17).

As Martin knelt in solitude on the roof of the priory church, looking in the direction of the blessed sacrament, he was embracing the entire world in the infinite spaciousness of his heart. In Martin's contemplation, the poor also tasted and saw that the Lord is good. Brother Fernando Aragonés, the head infirmarian, testified that "the two virtues of the active and contemplative life were so united in [Martin] that, when he would exercise charity by serving the sick, he did so with a spirit that was recollected, composed, and full of devotion. He was always present to the Creator, engaging and conversing with God in his soul…through the simplicity of his words and actions."[7]

Giuliana Cavallini, biographer of the lives of both Martin and Catherine, uses the story of Jesus' visit to the house of Martha and Mary (Lk 10:38–42) to capture beautifully the equilibrium that held Martin's contemplation and compassion together in a single unity. "In Martin's heart," she writes, "Martha and Mary never disputed, because Mary accompanied Martha always and everywhere. But when Martha had finished her work, Mary took Martin by the hand and led him to some hidden spot where he could enjoy the presence of the Lord, alone….Solitude drew Martin like a magnet."[8]

Most insightful is Cavallini's phrase, "Mary accompanied Martha always." In other words, Brother Martin's many hours of tireless service of the poor—in the streets of Malambo, caring for the sick in the infirmary, feeding the mice in the garden, healing the wounded dogs, visiting the African slaves, planting fig trees for the poor—were all done while his heart remained recollected in silent adoration. The truth is, he was *always* hidden in God's silent heart of love—even in the midst of long and tiring days of apostolic service. He never stopped breathing in the presence of God, and he never stopped breathing out compassion. It was all one. It was Martin's very life.

## REFLECTION QUESTIONS

How do I pray? Do I struggle with trying to balance my life between being present to God and present with the poor and needy? How might I hold the poor in the infinite spaciousness of my heart while I pray? Try cutting out a picture of someone from the newspaper, and then spend some time praying for that person and the many like him or her. What practical things can I do to stay "recollected" throughout the day? Experiment with setting aside fifteen minutes of silence each day. During the silence, be mindful of your breathing. As you breathe in, know that the Holy Spirit is coming in to fill your whole being (Jn 20:22), and as you breathe out, know that you are breathing out compassion upon the world. Practice this mindful breathing throughout the day.

## NOTES

1. Brother Herman de Porres Johnson, O.P., "A Fusion of Souls," *Martin's Message* 1998, vol. II, no. 2), p. 2. This is a publication of the Saint Martin de Porres Shrine in Memphis, Tennessee.

2. JAB, pp. 209, 224. This is a compilation of three separate testimonies.

3. Meister Eckhart, O.P., *Meister Eckhart: Sermons and Treatises*, ed. and trans. Maurice O'C. Walshe (Shaftesbury: Element Books, 1979), sermon nos. 1 and 6, pp. 6, 59.

4. Catherine of Siena, O.P., cited in Guiliana Cavallini, *Things Visible and Invisible,* trans. Mary Jeremiah, O.P. (New York: Alba House, 1996), p. 26.

5. Catherine of Siena, O.P, cited in Mary O'Driscoll, O.P., *Catherine of Siena: Passion for Truth, Compassion for Humanity* (New York: New City Press, 1993), pp. 115–116.

6. Bartolomé de las Casas, *History of the Indies*, translated and edited by Andrée Collard (New York: Harper & Row, 1971), III, p. 286.

7. JAB, p. 325. Testimony given by Brother Fernando Aragonés.

8. CAV, p. 153.

## TEN

# Room for All

## FOCUS: TOGETHER IN PEACE

Martin knew what it meant to be laughed at and discriminated against. During his lifetime, the European intellectuals were still debating whether the Indians, Africans, and mulattos in America were *full* human beings. Needless to say, this posed a faith dilemma for many of the victims of discrimination. They wondered if they could accept the God of a religion that approved of war, violence, and slavery against innocent people. There is a story told by Bartolomé de las Casas of an Indian who asked if the Spaniards were going to heaven. When he was told "yes," he responded that he would prefer, then, to go somewhere else. Martin, though, found in the open arms of the crucified Christ a God whose love knows no limits, and whose table is big enough so that the whole universe to sit down and eat.

*One of the friars from Martin's priory walked into a room near*
*the kitchen to find a strange sight. At Martin's feet were a dog*
*and a cat eating peacefully from the same bowl of soup. Suddenly*
*a little mouse stuck his head out from a hole in the wall. Martin,*
*without hesitation, spoke to the mouse, "Don't be afraid, little*
*one. If you're hungry come and eat with the others." The mouse*
*hesitated but then scampered to the bowl of soup from which the*
*dog and cat were eating. The friar who was watching all this*
*could not speak. Here before his eyes, at the feet of the mulatto*
*Saint Martin, a dog, a cat, and a mouse were eating from the*
*same bowl of soup, natural enemies eating peacefully side by side.*[1]

## MARTIN'S LITTLE WAY

García Rivera admits that these little stories about Martin's life
often deceive the specialists, giving the impression that they are
meant for children. This is unfortunate. It is true that Martin's
path to God was a kind of *little way*, a path of simple, uncompli-
cated faith, not so unlike that of the popular French Carmelite,
Saint Thérèse of Lisieux. The simple spirituality of both, though,
is not to be confused with a childish faith, lacking in depth. Quite
the contrary. Their little way—clear and transparent, like fresh
spring water—unfolds as a series of anecdotal stories which together form a narrative, in a way similar to the parables of Jesus.
They invite us to a faith response by engaging our hearts more
than our minds. Like Jesus' parables, the stories of Martin's life
are packed with gospel truth. Their simplicity *is* their strength.

One day a Canaanite woman approached Jesus and asked
him if he would heal her daughter, who was tormented by a de-
mon. The Canaanites were not Jews. She was a Gentile, a non-
believer. Jesus was not even supposed to speak to people like her.
At first he refused her request, saying, "I was sent only to the lost
sheep of the house of Israel." In other words, "You are from a
different tribe; I can't help you." He then used a harsh phrase: "It

is not fair to take the children's food (the food of the Jews) and throw it to the dogs (the gentiles)."[2] Concerned for her sick daughter, she had no choice but to persist: "Yes, Lord, yet even the dogs eat the crumbs that fall from their masters' table." Jesus was left speechless: "Woman, great is your faith! Let it be done for you as you wish." The girl was healed immediately (Mt 15:27–28).

If there were ever a gospel story that shows how Jesus grew and changed during his years of public ministry, it is this one. This story is vitally important if we are to understand the rest of Jesus' life, his message, the Last Supper, and his death. He lived within a culture and a religion that saw the Gentiles as enemies, unbelievers, godless heathens, not so different from how the Indians and Africans were viewed during the years of European colonialism in America.

The great *miracle* in this story is that Jesus does finally "break bread" with the Canaanite woman. He heals her *and* her daughter by establishing authentic *communion* with them, by reaching out and offering them the gift of life and love. He does not turn them away because of their religious differences, nor does he simply toss them the crumbs, as one would to a dog. He invites them to sit at the table of God's love.

This infuriated the religious leaders at the time, pulling out from under them their platform of power and domination. This is clearly seen on another occasion, when Jesus was eating a meal at Matthew's house, surrounded by people of questionable religious purity. The Pharisees, terribly upset, demanded an explanation from his disciples: "Why does your teacher eat with tax collectors and sinners?" (Mt 9:11). For Jesus, this posed absolutely no problem at all, because it was love—not purity—that was the guiding principle of his ministry.

This is exactly what is going on in the *little story* about Martin welcoming the dog, the cat, and the mouse to the same bowl of soup. He opened up a space within his servant heart for the outcasts to break bread together. This is no children's story. It is the gospel of Christ, pure and simple. It is a story about the all-inclusive love of God that breaks down the barriers that separate us from one another. Not only do the dog, the cat, and the mouse eat together, but Martin himself is part of their communion table. It is he who hosts the banquet.

For Saint Paul and his disciples, welcoming the Gentiles, the outsiders, into the family of God was one of the great, liberating gifts of the gospel: "In Christ Jesus you who were once far off have been brought near by the blood of Christ. For he is our peace; in his flesh he has made both groups into one and has broken down the dividing wall" (Eph 2:13–14). In Christ, there are no more walls, and no more crumbs thrown to the dogs (or the mice, for that matter!).

Martin understood this gospel truth with every fiber of his being. God's table is for everyone—and every living creature under the heavens. He who was a social outcast himself, knew that in Christ he was seated with dignity at the banquet table of God's reign (see Lk 14:21).

What about our world today? What would Martin say about a nation that spends millions of dollars on diet programs while millions of people starve today in our world? Who is missing from this table? How can a nation whose crops are picked and processed, whose restaurants are staffed, and whose hotel rooms and public restrooms are cleaned in large part by *Latino* immigrants deny these very same people a place at the table of justice? This spirit of welcome must begin with us who call ourselves followers of Jesus. The Catholic bishops of Mexico and the United States wrote recently in a joint letter, echoing words from Pope John Paul II, "In the church no one is a stranger....[We] welcome all persons regardless of race, culture, language, and nation with joy, charity, and hope....We stand with you, our migrant brothers and sisters, and we will continue to advocate on your behalf for just and fair migration policies."[3]

What about the community of world religions? Do we sit at the table of dialogue and mutual respect with Muslims, Protestants, Jews, Buddhists, Hindus, and others? Do we pray with people of other faith traditions? Sister Pascaline Coff, O.S.B., says that dialogue with people of other faiths is "a form of the practice of hospitality...welcoming the Divine in the other."[4]

This is what Jesus did with the Canaanite woman, and what Martin did with the mouse; they offered hospitality: "I was a stranger and you welcomed me" (Mt 25:35). Dorothy Day, founder of the Catholic Worker movement in the U.S., said that we offer hospitality to the poor "not because it *might be* Christ... but because they *are* Christ....We start by loving them for him, and soon we love them for themselves, each one a unique person."[5]

How, then, do we offer hospitality to all the people who "don't fit" into the dominant, acceptable categories that our world sets up? Are the handicapped visible in our world? Where are the mentally ill? Is the political refugee offered safe haven? Do we remember that criminals are human beings, and need a place for healing and rehabilitation? Mother Teresa of Calcutta once said, after visiting the men on death row at San Quentin Prison in California, "Whatever you do to [the least of] these men, you do to God."

And in our churches, synagogues, and temples? Who is missing? Who does not feel welcomed? Is there a place for the deaf in our religious services? Do those who have suffered the tragedy of divorce know that they have a place at the table of the Eucharist? What about gay men and lesbians? Do we just throw them the crumbs as if they were dogs? Where are the single mothers and fathers? the pregnant teens? the elderly? Are they seated at the table?

Several years ago a middle-aged man, dying of AIDS, showed up at a Catholic hospital that had a special hospice for those with HIV-AIDS. He had lived in the street for many years; he was dirty, hungry, hurting. He was given a bath, a clean bed, food, and good care. He had been a practicing Catholic many years before, but his life had taken unexpected turns, and he had wandered from the faith. One day he got up from his bed and went to the chapel for Mass. It had been awhile, but suddenly, after a long time, he wanted to *see God* again. He listened to the priest's homily and felt happy to once again be in God's house, safe from the violent streets. It came time for Communion, and with his cane he got in line to receive the body and blood of Christ. When he had almost reached the priest, someone grabbed him and pulled him from the line, telling him that he was not prepared to receive the Lord, that he needed to go to confession first. He walked back to his seat confused and sad. He had so hoped to *see God* again.[6]

> Martin, without hesitation, spoke to the mouse, "Don't be afraid, little one. If you're hungry come and eat with the others."

## REFLECTION QUESTIONS

Make a list of people you know who feel "left out, overlooked, forgotten, pushed aside, not included." Take some time to pray for each one of them. Read one or both of the following texts: Matthew 15:21–28 or Luke 14:14–24. What do these texts say about "God's table"? How does our nation exclude or include people at the table of justice? How might I help to make at least one person feel more welcomed at "God's table"?

## NOTES

1. AGR, p. 4. This testimony comes from the head infirmarian, Fernando Aragonés.
2. It is strangely coincidental that the Jews used the same degrading word "dogs" when speaking of the Gentiles that was used to insult Martin. He was frequently called a "mulatto dog."
3. The Bishops of Mexico and the United States, *Strangers No Longer: Together on a Journey of Hope*, January 2003, #103–106. The letter was published in *Origins* (February 6, 2003).

4. Pascaline Coff, O.S.B., "Merton's Message for Contemporary Contemplatives," a talk given at the annual Merton dinner in Tulsa, Oklahoma (December 4, 2003).
5. Dorothy Day, "An Appetite for God," by Patrick Jordan, *Commonweal* (October 24, 1997), p. 15.
6. This is a true story.

## ELEVEN

# Joyful Nonviolence

### FOCUS: LOVE EVEN THOSE WHO HATE YOU

"God created the world in marvelous diversity, a garden of fe-
cund asymmetries."[1] Unfortunately, not everyone experiences this
garden of diversity as something so "marvelous." The color of
Martin's skin provided the needed scapegoat for certain people to
project their own self-hatred onto someone else. Hitler, of course,
turned this sickness into an art form, but we see it in our own day
when nations, religions, and political parties demonize one another. We see it when anti-immigration laws seek to drive the
"stranger in our midst" underground. Hatred comes disguised in
many forms. Martin de Porres, however, refused to play the game
of hatred. He refused to respond to violence with violence. Instead, he teaches us the way to disarm our hatred through the
practice of love.

*Some of the religious brothers called Martin a "perro mulato" (a mulatto dog), along with other names aimed at upsetting him or causing him to get angry. Martin never showed anger. In fact, he would respond with a joyful smile, telling them that what they said was right and that they really knew him well. Martin would then serve these very ones who attacked him with even greater love.*[2]

## TEACHING THE POWER OF LOVE

This is an example of how the "little stories" about Martin's life turn the world upside down. It is a real tragedy that for many centuries these *mulatto dog* stories (they are quite numerous) have been recounted as if Martin were proposing that oppressed people hang their heads low and take the lashes from the master's whip with humility. To read these stories in this way is to drive a stake into the heart of Martin de Porres, for nothing could be further from the truth. His entire life was spent lifting God's poor and beaten children out of the violence of hatred.

Others simply skirt around these uncomfortable stories of Martin thanking people for treating him like a dog and kissing the feet of those who despised him. We cannot be true to Martin by ignoring these stories, dismissing them as nothing but examples of old-fashioned and unhealthy humility. This approach furthers the caricature of Martin as an ignorant pawn of an oppressive religion and, worse yet, misses the power hidden like a seed in the stories themselves.

Martin was no dummy. He was so on fire with love that he could face his enemies with patience until they finally surrendered to the power of love. This is the key to the practice of nonviolence. Long before Mahatma Gandhi and Martin Luther King, Jr., systematized the philosophy and practice of active nonviolence, what Gandhi called *ahimsa*, Martin had already learned the basics from his dialogues with the gentle Christ on the cross, and from his prayerful listening to the gospel. The words of Jesus were quite clear: "I give you a new commandment, that you love one another. Just as I have loved you, you also should love one another" (Jn 13:34).

To love *just as Jesus loved*; Martin knew that this was no easy task. Daily, though, he worked at putting into practice this *new* commandment of his gentle Christ. Many years later, another proponent of nonviolence, César Chávez, who spent his life struggling on behalf of farm workers, spoke about the price one pays when committed to this path: "Nonviolence exacts a very high price from one who practices it....[It] takes more guts, if I can put it bluntly, than violence." It took *guts* and patient endurance for Martin to look into the hateful eyes of those who called him a "mulatto dog" and offer them the healing that comes from authentic love and understanding. Again in the words of Chávez, "Nonviolence in action is a very potent force and it can't be stopped....If we have the capacity to endure, if we have the patience, things will change."[3]

We can only understand Martin's strange responses to the violence inflicted upon him and others if we see him as a teacher, as one who used the practice of nonviolence and patient endurance to teach others that *there must be another way*. Martin, of course, would laugh if he heard us calling him a teacher, just as he would with the title of preacher. He had no such pretense. But that is precisely what he was. He scrubbed toilets instead of spending his days in the archbishop's palace precisely to *teach* Father Juan to reevaluate the priorities in his own life. He prepared a salad of capers for Father Pedro Montes de Oca, who had just called him a "mulatto dog and other bad things," to lead him into a new way of dealing with his anger. Anyone who has lived in community or been married knows that such a nonviolent approach to the little "violences" of daily life is no easy path to walk. Martin did not enjoy being treated like an animal anymore than Jesus enjoyed being crucified. Both, though, had "the capacity to endure" with the hope and trust that love would ultimately triumph.

To our bitterest opponents we say: We shall match your
capacity to inflict suffering by our capacity to endure suffering. We shall meet your physical force with soul force.
Do to us what you will, we shall continue to love you.…
Throw us in jail, we shall still love you. Send your hooded
perpetrators of violence into our community at the midnight hour and beat us and leave us half-dead and we
shall still love you. One day we will win freedom, but not
only for ourselves. We shall so appeal to your heart and
conscience that we shall win you in the process.[4]

These words, of course, are from *the other Martin*—Martin
Luther King, Jr.—and they very beautifully reveal the power hidden in the practice of nonviolence. It is a spiritual path enfleshed
in love, and its only goal is to win the opponent over to love. As
the story with which we began this chapter said, "Martin would
then serve these very ones who attacked him with even greater
love."

Limatambo was a large *hacienda* (farm) owned by the Dominicans on the outskirts of Lima.[5] Martin spent much time there
planting medicinal herbs and olive trees, as well as visiting with
the poor indigenous and African farm workers who lived there.
One night some of the friars found Martin in the barn, feeding
the mules and the oxen. "Leave that work for the Blacks," they
told him. Martin responded, "The Blacks are tired and the animals have worked more than I have. They have earned their food,
and it would be a lack of charity not to give it to them. I, on the
other hand, have done nothing to serve God today; I do this so
that the day will not pass without doing something for God's
holy service."[6]

This is Martin, the teacher of nonviolent love at his best. He
easily could have berated the friars, calling them "racist pigs"
and unworthy servants of the gospel. After all, do the Scriptures
not say, "eye for eye, tooth for a tooth"? (Ex 21:24). What he did
instead was act in such a way that his example might serve as a

teaching about love. Nonviolence, Gandhi frequently said, is not about being victorious over the enemy, but about inviting them to conversion.[7] The friars that found Martin in the barn that night knew very well that Martin had done much to serve God that day. He was playing a secret game with them, *teasing* them into conversion: "I do this so that the day will not pass without doing something for God's holy service." Martin's heart smiled as he said these words, for who, after all, was letting the day pass without doing something holy for God? Martin was a wise teacher; he wanted to lure his brothers' hearts into the "trap of love." As the *other Martin* said many years later with such eloquence: "We shall so appeal to your heart and conscience that we shall win you in the process." In the end, it is all about love.

## REFLECTION QUESTIONS
Begin by reading Matthew 5:38–48. If possible, spend some time with this pivotal teaching of Jesus (part of his sermon on the mount), following it up with some journaling if possible. What is Jesus saying? What are the consequences of this teaching for us today? Is there any "enemy" lurking in your life these days who might need a second chance? How does a nation that develops and sells arms respond to this teaching of Jesus? What might it mean—in very concrete terms—to love violent criminals, even terrorists? How do we respond from a faith perspective so that we can *love those who hate* into conversion? Reread the Martin Luther King, Jr., quote on page 68 and end with a prayer.

## NOTES

1. AGR, p. 100.
2. JAB, p. 179. Told by Antonio Gutiérrez, O.P.
3. The César Chávez quotes are used with the permission of the César Chávez Foundation, P.O. Box 62, Keene, CA 93531.
4. Martin Luther King, Jr., *Strength to Love.*
5. Limatambo was also a place where the older friars went to rest and convalesce from illnesses, and the novices enjoyed a respite from the rigors of life at the priory. The farm workers, many of whom were black, looked forward to Martin's frequent visits as a source of great joy. Martin was one of them, and they respected him like a father. He healed their wounds, corrected them when it was needed, educated them in the Catholic faith, and arbitrated their family quarrels. He also joined in when they were celebrating their *fiestas.*
6. JAB, p. 281.
7. Mahatma Gandhi, *Gandhi on Non-Violence*, edited and introduction by Thomas Merton (New York: New Directions, 1964), pp. 25, 33.

## TWELVE

# Spiritual Father

## FOCUS: PARENT TO THE POOR

Even though Martin was not a priest, and therefore was addressed as "Fray Martín" ("Brother Martin"), there were many people who insisted on calling Martin "father." Once, while visiting some farms near Limatambo, some Indians approached and asked Martin if he would celebrate a Mass in memory of their deceased parents and grandparents. Martin immediately said *"Hijos, yo no soy de misa"* ("My children, I do not celebrate the Mass."), to which the Indians responded, "No problem, *Padre*, we know that you will have the Masses celebrated."[1] The truth is, of course, that Martin *was* very much a father. He poured out his life in love as a gift to others. He who was "son of an unknown father" became the spiritual father of many.

*"Brother Martin was a man of great charity, who...healed his brother religious when they were sick but also assisted in the larger duty of spreading the Great Love of the world. For this they knew him as their father and consolation, calling him 'father of the poor.' Moreover, he cared for lay people outside [these walls] from every state of life, healing them of their pains, wounds and inflammations...and thus an infinite number sought him out and all found in him some help: the sick, relief; the afflicted, consolation; and the rest, refuge. He did this willingly, his semblance happy and peaceful."*

*Friar Antonio Gutiérrez, O.P.*[2]

## NURTURING OTHERS ON THE WAY

In the early centuries of the Church, many men and women went out into the desert to live ascetical lives of penance and prayer, the most famous of them being Anthony of Egypt. These "desert fathers and mothers" sought simplicity and solitude in order to live the gospel in a radical way, as a sign of the coming of the kingdom of God. It was common for Christians longing to live a deeper life of prayer and discipleship to seek out these desert fathers and mothers for counsel and guidance on the spiritual path. Martin, though he would never have said it himself, was a "spiritual father" in this ancient desert tradition. His love and wisdom nurtured and guided others along the path of life.

Martin always called the blacks and Indians "hijos" ("my children"), and because of this filial love, he often found himself in situations in which he had to protect and defend the poor, as fathers and mothers do with their children. One day someone stole the mattress and blanket of a black man who was one of Martin's helpers in the infirmary. Upon hearing of it, Martin immediately said, "You stay here," and then he went directly to the cell of one of the friars, where he found the stolen articles. Scolding the friar for not keeping a better eye on the priory servant who had stolen the things, Martin said: "Father, if your servant does not have a bed, then buy him one. He shouldn't be going and stealing one from someone else." Martin picked the mattress up and carried it back to his helper.[3]

Martin's friend, Juan Vásquez, tells another story of two delinquents taking refuge in the priory, trying to escape from possible arrest by the Royal Court. The officials eventually suspected that the two men might be hiding in the basement beneath the infirmary kitchen of the priory, and so, says Juan, "At two-thirty in the afternoon Don Cristóbal de la Cerda arrived in search of the two delinquents...who fled up through the infirmary kitchen to Brother Martin's cell. 'Father, for the love of God, help us,' they cried. ' The Justice is after us; they are already here.' Martin responded, 'Come in here; get on your knees and pray to God.' They knelt down just as the Court official entered the cell. Martin also knelt down—in front of the delinquents. The official looked around, and seeing nothing but some mattresses on the floor, turned and left."[4] God had miraculously granted them mercy (and invisibility!).

Busto notes, in his comments on this incident, that Martin acted in defense of the right to religious asylum. The Court official, he notes, far from exercising his authority, was actually abusing it, by entering illegally into a sacred space. Though there is no record of the words Martin said to the men whose lives God saved that day, we can be sure that he let them know that next time they were on their own! However, after such a powerful experience of God's mercy, and thanks to the help of "Padre Martín," there probably was no "next time."

Another incident shows the depth of respect that some of Lima's upper class had for Martin. Doctor Baltazar Carranza de Orozco, a Spaniard, was a lawyer for the Royal Court. His reverence and love for Martin were so great that he begged him for several years to accept him as a spiritual son, and to permit him to call Martin "*Padre*." Martin resisted for a long time, saying in his typical fashion, "Why would you want a mulatto for a father?"

So insistent was the doctor that Martin finally gave in to his request. A few days later he found Doctor Carranza in the sacristy, walked up to him, embraced him, and called him "son." Then, with a bit of humor, Martin added, "That means that your children are now my grandchildren." Doctor Carranza testified that from 1628 onward, "our friendship continued to grow."[5]

Martin's closest lay friend seems to have been his helper and traveling companion, Juan Vásquez de Parra. Juan, who was born in Spain, came to America in 1635 with his father, an official of the Holy Office of the Inquisition. Soon after arriving in Lima, Juan's father died, leaving Juan, only about fourteen at the time, to survive on his own. Not long after that, Martin found him wandering around the priory cemetery one day, "poor and tattered." Martin immediately took Juan up to his cell and gave him a clean shirt to put on. He then explained to the young lad that he was welcome to take his meals at the priory and that he could sleep in the linen room that was adjacent to Martin's cell. Martin also encouraged him to spend a few days looking around the priory to see if there might be a trade he would like to learn. Juan, whom Martin affectionately nicknamed *"Juancho,"* soon let it be known that he wanted to be a barber/surgeon—like Martin—and thus began the friendship that deeply graced Martin's final three or four years of life.

Juan always referred to Martin as *"Padre,"* and indeed Martin cared for him like a son. When one looks back at the gift of this friendship in the context of Martin's life, one cannot help but see the wondrous hand of God at work. The spiritual father-son relationship that Martin shared with his friend Juan was the coming to full circle of Martin's journey with his own father, who, we can assume, had died by this time, still estranged from his son.

Juancho was, in a mysterious way, a blending of both Martin and his father. Like Martin, Juancho was a "son without a father," but he was also Spanish—fashioned from the same clay as Martin's father. In Juancho, Martin and his father, who was, incidentally, also named Juan, finally met face to face: a duel between two warriors. This was no ordinary duel, though; it was a spiritual battle of two hearts finally becoming one in the heart of Christ. "He is our peace; in his flesh he has made both groups into one and has broken down the dividing wall, that is, the hostility between us" (Eph 2:14).

This time, though, the gospel story reversed the characters, with the prodigal father coming home to the son, and being received with the kiss of peace that heals all wars. Juancho was the missing piece of a puzzle that Martin's heart had longed to find— the end of a journey that had always seemed unfinished. By loving Juancho as his son, Martin found the catalyst for a healing on many levels. He was able to become the father he never had, a father who reached out in compassion to an orphaned son and, in so doing, Martin loved the son whom his own father had failed. At the same time, by Martin's reaching out in unconditional love to Juancho, a Spaniard, he was, in a spiritual sense, reaching out to heal his own father's wounded heart. In this mystery, which is none other than the paschal mystery, God redeemed Juan de Porras through the courageous, all-embracing love of his son.

Perhaps this was Martin's greatest miracle—a free gift from God, given to him during the last four years of his life.

## REFLECTION QUESTIONS

Do I share my spiritual life with a wisdom figure, a spiritual mother or father? Have I ever been a guide for someone else on the journey of life? What were some of Martin's gifts that made him such a wise spiritual father? List them. Do I have any of these same qualities? Why was the friendship with Juancho such a source of joy for Martin? How did this spiritual friendship with Juancho bring the relationship between Martin and his father to a place of healing and peace? Pray for the reconciliation between families and nations.

## NOTES

1. JAB, p. 303.
2. AGR, p. 2. This testimony was given as part of Martin's beatification process. JAB, p. 124.
3. JAB, p. 282.
4. JAB, p. 284.
5. JAB, p. 180. Doctor Carranza gave this testimony himself.

## THIRTEEN

# Martin's Death

### FOCUS: A LIFE FREELY GIVEN

Martin's death was to Lima what Mother Teresa of Calcutta's death was to the world. It was an event which moved an entire people, a whole city—the passing of a great saint. Thomas Merton once wrote, "In my ending is my meaning."[1] Martin's ending, his final days, the throngs who gathered to bid him farewell, all attest to the meaning of his life. It was a great life, one well-lived. In the end, Martin, like Jesus, gave his life away—freely—as a gift: "The good shepherd lays down his life for the sheep....No one takes it from me, but I lay it down of my own accord" (Jn 10:11,18). And so he did, on November 3, 1639.

*"The end came. It all began when Martin was saying good-bye to Juan Vásquez de Parra, who had become a soldier and was about to embark as part of the Armada of the South Sea. Martin said to him in [the port of] Callao, 'Adios, Juancho. We will not see each*

*other again in this century, and if we were to see each other, you would doubt.' Having said these words, Juan departed and Martin stayed....This was around June 1639. Three months went by and in the third or fourth week of October Martin fell ill."*[2]

## WISDOM FOR THE WORLD

Martin knew that the end was near. What cannot go unnoticed is how the beginning of the end coincided with Juancho's good-bye. His "son" was a man now, a free man, like Martin himself. The experience of spiritual fatherhood was, for Martin, the culminating grace of his life. Now, with Juancho's setting sail for the East and the adventures of life that awaited him, Martin knew that he, too, was ready for his final journey: the preparation for death.

Like a good father, Martin had passed on to his son the wisdom of his own lived experience. He had poured out his own life into the heart and soul of Juancho, just like Christ had done with him. "I do not call you servants any longer....I have called you friends, because I have made known to you everything that I have heard from my Father. You did not choose me but I chose you. And I appointed you to go and bear fruit, fruit that will last" (Jn 15:15–16). Martin's life was complete. Now it was time to let go.

Each night the Dominican friars had the custom of gathering in the priory chapel to end their day with the Compline liturgy[3] and the singing of two ancient canticles. One of them, the *Salve, Regina*, was sung to Mary, the mother of mercy. The other canticle, from Luke's Gospel, was the Canticle of Simeon—an old Hebrew man's song of thanks to God for letting his tired, old eyes see the fulfillment of God's promise to Israel before he died. One can imagine Martin returning from the port of Callao that June day in 1639, after saying good-bye to his beloved Juancho. He must have felt the same mixture of emotions—joy, pride, sadness—that any parent feels when a son or daughter leaves home for the first time. There he was, back in the chapel where he had spent many nights in prayer, joining the friars and old Simeon in giving thanks to God and praying for the grace needed for the final journey:

"Master, now you are dismissing your servant in peace,
    according to your word;
for my eyes have seen your salvation,
    which you have prepared in the presence
    of all the peoples" (Lk 2:29–31).

With these words, Martin began to prepare for death. The first day of his illness (he probably died of typhus), Martin told his friend, Father Juan de Barbarán, who had stopped by to see him, "The time has come. I will die of this illness, and no medicine is going to be of any help." Martin never wavered from this conviction, and each time the friars showed up with medicines with which to save the life of their dear and holy brother, Martin refused. As was noted earlier, he even scolded them for proposing to kill animals in order to make medicines for his healing. He walked into the arms of death with utter freedom, overflowing with gratitude for God's gifts of life and love. In the words of a contemporary Dominican friar in Peru, "Martin loved life. He adored life. He defended life."[4]

Within three months, Martin was bedridden. He did not stop being "Martin" though. He tried to resist letting the friars put sheets on his bed, but the prior commanded him to accept under obedience. It was a trick he had tried once before, when struck with a case of severe fevers. That time Martin had insisted on sleeping on his scrap of cowhide on the cold floor, even after the prior had ordered that a mattress and sheets be taken to his room. Martin finally accepted the mandate—faithful, at least in theory, to his vow of obedience. It was all useless, however, because they later discovered that, though Martin was "obediently sleeping on the mattress and sheets," he was doing so while still dressed in his penitential hair shirt and woolen habit. Arguing with Martin's stubborn holiness was a waste of time.

As the end drew near, Martin received the anointing of the sick and the sacrament of confession "with many tears." He also received the *Viaticum*, the final Eucharist, a Latin term which means "the provision for the journey." The bread he had broken and shared with so many during his life was now given to him as bread for the journey. In a way similar to the final hours of life of the founder of the Order, his holy father, Saint Dominic, Martin even spoke some words to those who were gathered, "which brought all who were present to tears." Early in the evening of November 3, another of his old friends, Francisco Ortiz, arrived. Years later he shared his final, tender moments with Martin: "I wanted to say good-bye in case he died that night," he recalled. Approaching the bed, he bent over and kissed Martin on the neck. Martin, feeling the presence of his friend, "reached his arm out and rubbed my head and neck....He then drew me close to him with great strength, pressing me against his neck so much that I began to sweat profusely." At that moment, Francisco remembered, as did many others, "There was a heavenly aroma softer and greater than anything I had ever experienced."

> Be kind to one another, tenderhearted, forgiving...imitators of God, as beloved children, and live in love, as Christ loved us and gave himself up for us, a fragrant offering and sacrifice to God (Eph 4:32—5:2).

Twice that evening they asked Martin if it was time to sound the *tablas*, the wooden clappers used to summon the community to the bedside of a dying friar, and both times he shook his head "no." Finally, around eight o'clock that night, Martin was again asked, and this time, "lowering his head, he said 'yes.'" The friars gathered and began to sing the Creed and to say the prayers of commendation for the dying. Martin quietly breathed his last, surrounded by those who had been his brothers for forty-five years. The bells of the *convento*—the very ones that Martin had devotedly rung for more than four decades—announced to all of Lima that their beloved Martin had gone home to God, carrying in his heart the bread of life.

Bishop Pierre Claverie, O.P., the slain archbishop of Oran, Algeria, once said, "The value of my life depends on my capacity to give it away." Is this not what Martin teaches us so gently, so perfectly? His life was of such immense value because he gave it away, like bread—blessed and broken—every day of his life.

At his funeral the next day, the whole city of Lima was present, "people of every race, language and way of life." It was just what Martin would have wanted—a gathering around the eucharistic table where everyone has a place, where no one is left out. We can be sure that even the dogs and the cats and the mice were present that day, to say good-bye to the friend who had first invited them to "the table," the friend who, like Jesus, celebrated the end of his life by giving himself away. Martin's final gift was to become bread for the world.

## REFLECTION QUESTIONS

Why was Martin able to approach death so gently, with such great trust? Do I ever think about death? Does it frighten me, or do I feel at peace with dying? Jesus gave his life away. Martin gave his life away. Bishop Claverie gave his life away. Am I giving my life away little by little? How is giving one's life away a preparation for death? How do love, friendship, and marriage prepare us for death? Have you ever tried to write your own obituary or chosen the readings and music for your own funeral? You may want to try this, and reflect on the experience.

## NOTES

1. Thomas Merton, "The Night of Destiny," *Collected Poems* (New York: New Directions, 1977), p. 635.
2. JAB, p. 329. Most of the details of Martin's final days and death (including several of the quotes in this chapter) come from JAB, pp. 321–348.
3. Compline is the last *office*, or celebration of the divine liturgy each day in religious and monastic communities. While it is a preparation for sleep and the night, it also symbolizes one's preparation for death.
4. Guillermo Alvarez, O.P., *Historia de la Orden Dominicana en el Perú: Siglo XVII,* (Lima: Dominicans of Peru, 1977), vol. 1, p. 236.

## FOURTEEN

# Ordinary Holiness

### FOCUS: ENERGIZED BY GRACE

How does a person begin to pattern his or her own life on a life like Martin's without feeling overwhelmed? As a friend commented recently, "Martin did it all—from ringing bells and cleaning toilets to healing the sick, feeding the hungry, and blanketing the hills with herbs for the poor! And on top of all that, he spent half the night in prayer. How can we, ordinary laypeople—husbands and wives, parents and children, friends and coworkers—even come close to practicing our faith like Martin de Porres?" It is a good question. Certainly, the last thing that Martin would want is for us to feel "overwhelmed" by his life, and therefore paralyzed in our own following of Christ. How, then, can we be energized by his holy life, finding in his story a link with our own story? Let us return for a moment to the beginning of Martin's story.

*Martin asked Isabel García for a wax candle, or a stub of one....Afraid of a fire, but mostly wanting to know what was happening, Isabel allowed herself to be tempted by curiosity. Drawing near to the young boy's room, she peered through the cracks in the door. What she saw deeply moved her. Martin was on his knees, quiet, silent, and praying before an image of the Crucified. His dark silhouette was piously outlined against the glow of the candle, and such was this scene of prayerful anointing that it seemed almost impossible for such a young child.*[1]

## LIGHT OF CHRIST

A wax candle. A stub of a simple wax candle. With that, Martin began his long and beautiful journey to God. Actually, he had already begun the journey—with another candle—though he was not old enough at the time to remember it; it was just a day or two after his birth. He was carried in the arms of his mother and his godparents to the Church of San Sebastián in Lima for the sacrament of baptism. On that day a candle was lighted and Martin heard these words: "Receive the light of Christ, *lumen Christi.*" It was on *that* day that Martin's beautiful journey began to unfold.

The next sixty years all had something to do with that baptismal candle, which was an extension of the paschal light of Christ. Martin's light was not the blazing prophetic fire of Elijah, John the Baptist, or Joan of Arc. He was not a martyred missionary, remembered for carrying the light of the faith to faraway lands, though he dreamed of such a vocation. He did not build churches or orphanages; he was not a bishop or a pope, and did not found a religious congregation like Dominic, Francis, and Mother Teresa. Martin's light was more like a candle, simple, always burning, always shining into some dark corner of our suffering world. Martin's holiness was really quite ordinary.

Part of what "overwhelms" us four hundred years after

Martin's life is that the stories told about him seem so "big." He worked miracles, communicated with animals and lived on bread and boiled vegetables. We must remember, though, that these stories represent the image of a saintly life in that particular time in history. That is why it is so important to go *into* the stories of Martin's life, to *see* and *hear* the details that are *not* extraordinary. This requires a kind of holy curiosity, a keen eye for what seems insignificant, what is only hinted at and mentioned in passing. *That* is where we glimpse the masterpiece of Martin's holy life, and *that* is where we find the tiny candle burning brightly in the midst of the darkness.

Let us recall, for a moment, the story of Martin planting the branch of a fig tree on a hill in Amancaes—the same one that Juancho found budding eighteen days later. A miracle! Yes, it does seem to be a miracle. Why, though, are we so struck by the "miracle" of the tree budding so quickly? Why does the *out-of-the-ordinary* fascinate us so much? Do we think that holiness is out of the ordinary, too? What about Martin's words: "Thanks be to God, within two or three years it will bear fruit for the poor who pass by this way."[2] Is it not a miracle when someone does something as thoughtful as plant a fruit tree for the poor of future generations? Is that not the real miracle of love?

Saint Paul said, "If I speak in the tongues of mortals and of angels, but do not have love, I am a noisy gong or a clanging cymbal. And if I have prophetic powers...and if I have all faith, so as to remove mountains, but do not have love, I am nothing" (1 Cor 13:1–2). Maybe Saint Paul would say this of Martin's fig tree: "If I plant fig trees on every hilltop in the world, and do not have love, then I am nothing." But if I plant *one* fig tree so that the poor have something to eat, *that* is a great miracle indeed. It is the miracle of love. It may be a bit less heroic than our fascination with the extraordinary stuff, but is it less important? Is this not what the gospel of Jesus is all about?

Martin's life can seem *overwhelmingly holy* if we get caught up in the exterior signs and miss the *real* holiness behind the signs:

the holiness of love. Perhaps we have complicated the life of the saints more than is necessary. Maybe we have tried too hard to *look* like them, rather than *love* like them. Martin just went about his life loving one person and one dog at a time. Now *that* does not seem so difficult. It actually seems possible, almost enjoyable.

Maybe Martin actually *enjoyed* being in love with the world! Is that what he is trying to teach us? After all, it is no fun being angry, bitter, and self-centered, even though we spend a lot of time *being* that way. Is this not what is behind the story of Father Pedro Montes de Oca, who yelled at Martin and called him a mulatto dog (and a few other things)? Martin, we remember, left the room laughing, and then went to the kitchen and made him his favorite salad of capers. What a miracle! Who would have ever thought that making a caper salad could be such a wonderful miracle? Maybe we could all become saints! Imagine, a world full of caper salads made by holy people! It could be the beginning of a real revolution.

Martin was the kind of saint that reminds us that the miracle of love happens in the ordinary stuff of every day: sharing a salad and some bread with a friend, brewing a bit of chamomile tea for a stranger who is sick, planting a fig tree for the poor. Nothing too terribly heroic. It brings to mind the bumper sticker which reads: "Practice random acts of kindness." That is what Martin did. He walked through life with his stub of a candle in his hand and heart and practiced random acts of kindness. That is why he is a saint. In the end, maybe being a saint is not so difficult after all. Perhaps it is all really very ordinary—the miracle of loving here and now, today, in this very world in which I live.

We have all received the light of Christ through our baptism, and, like Martin, it is this light which guides us along the path of holiness. It need not be a fiery torch of extraordinary saintliness. Martin seemed rather happy with his candle stubs. In the words of the Christopher movement: "It is better to light one candle than curse the darkness." Holiness is God's light shining through a person's ordinary kindness.

Holiness is not a fig tree that blossoms miraculously; it is cutting some flowers from my garden and taking them to my neighbor who is undergoing a new round of chemotherapy. Holiness is not communicating with a dog, a cat, and a mouse in coded animal language, but serving a meal each week at the local soup kitchen or inviting a man who is living with HIV to join the family for dinner. Holiness is not spending entire nights in prayer, but living with a prayerful heart when I am driving to work or speaking with my teenage children about the dangers of drugs.

Holiness is small things done with love. Mother Teresa, surrounded by the squalor of the slums of Calcutta, decided to make of her life "something beautiful for God." That is what holiness is. Cooking a pot of soup for a neighbor is "something beautiful for God," as is sharing a gentle smile with a classmate who is sad. Healing is love enfleshed; this is what Martin did so well. He was a healer because he was a lover. And because he was both, he was a saint. Maybe being holy is not so complicated after all.

### REFLECTION QUESTIONS

How was Martin's saintly life *ordinary* (or do I tend to look only at the extraordinary virtues of the saints)? What are the ordinary things that I do each day (make a list)? How might I love others in these daily activities? Is there someone in particular who needs a miracle of love? When I look out at the world, with all its problems and suffering, is there *one* act of loving kindness that I can do to help God's miracle become more of a reality? Martin planted a fig tree for the poor. What can I do as one of God's saints-in-process?

### NOTES
1. JAB, p. 59.
2. JAB, p. 300.

## FIFTEEN

# Solidarity With the Poor

## FOCUS: THE FAITH OF DOÑA PAULINA[1]

There is rarely a church in Latin America that does not have a statue of Saint Martin de Porres, usually surrounded by candles—like the ones Martin used during his night vigils as a child. Revered throughout the continent, Martin's message, like that of the much-loved Virgin of Guadalupe, is one of hope, solidarity, and God's special love for the poor. Devotion to Martin de Porres reaches from Ireland to Vietnam, and is found in many parts of Africa, and the United States, as well. His simple life of prayer and compassion is easily understood by those seeking a deeper spiritual life. This final chapter in our fifteen days is a true story, and shows how Martin lives today in the faith of the poorest of the poor, revealing to all of us the loving face of God.

*Doña Paulina is a poor woman who has been on the same street corner in Lima, Peru, selling newspapers for more than thirty years. She is a small woman, but strong, with streaks of gray beginning to show in her hair. Her permanently chapped skin tells its own story of hardship. The daughter of Quechua Indians,[2] Paulina left her mountain village many years ago to begin a new life in a foreign land: the city of Lima. She not only had to find a job that would support her, but she also was forced to begin learning Spanish. Her family and all the people of her Andean village spoke Quechua, so she had never had to learn Spanish. She did not have the luxury of combining her work with going to school; she had never been to school. So she worked to survive, and later to raise her children. The tragic irony is that Doña Paulina cannot even read the newspapers that she sells.*

*I met Doña Paulina when I was a theology student in Lima in 1985. Our Dominican community bought the daily paper from her, at her little makeshift stand on the street corner. We became friends. She affectionately called me "hermanito" (little brother). Her smile, though always marked by a slight shadow of suffering, has always been radiant and full of love. We chatted each morning as my Dominican brothers and I waited for the bus on our way to classes. Our's was the orange #57 bus, and as we boarded it each day, engulfed in its cloud of smoke and fumes, the last thing I'd hear was, "Chao, hermanito! Que le vaya bien!"[3] I was headed to quiet classrooms to read and study theology, while she sat there on her wooden stool for fourteen hours a day, burned by the sun, bombarded by noise and breathing in the fumes of hundreds of buses and cars. Then, as now, those fourteen hours earn her about a dollar or two a day.*

*I have returned to Peru many times over the years, and one of the first things I do when I get to the city is go over and see my friend, Doña Paulina. After almost twenty years now, when she sees me coming down the street, she still waves and smiles as if I were just returning from one of my theology classes. Since meeting Paulina, I have been to dozens of countries and thousands of cities, while she has sat on this very same corner every single day. Sometimes it simply boggles my mind. The poor are not only poor economically, but their minds are impoverished by the enslaving lack of possibilities in life. I am reminded of the phrase of the United Negro College Fund, "A mind is a terrible thing to waste." It is so true.*

*I was in Peru recently to teach a course to young Peruvian Dominicans—and, of course, to visit dear Paulina. For me, to return every few years to Doña Paulina's corner and have a long talk with this woman of such profound faith and holiness grounds me. This woman has been one of the greatest spiritual teachers in my life, though she, like Martin de Porres, would laugh at so outlandish a suggestion. Her life is too transparent and too occupied with survival for such ideas.*

*During the first of our several conversations during this visit, I asked Doña Paulina about her children. Two of them have been in prison for almost ten years now—yet another heavy pain in her already heavy heart. Each time that I have seen Paulina during these ten years, she has recounted the way she saves up her money, penny by penny, so that she can take the two-day bus ride to the southern town of Puno, in order to spend one day with her sons, only to begin the long, two day trip home: four days of travel, one day of visiting, and five days of missed work. Each trip adds a couple more years to her tired body.*

*"How are your sons in Puno faring?" I asked on this visit. "Have you been able to travel there lately?" She looked up at me with a sly smile on her face, which caught me completely by surprise. Typically, she talks about these two sons with tears in her eyes. "They have both been moved to prisons in Lima now," she said, "so I can visit them more frequently. You know, 'hermanito,' I am getting old and it is very difficult for me to make that trip." I was elated. At least one small part of her daily suffering was finally relieved. "Thanks be to God!" I exclaimed. "How did that happen?" Her eyes still dancing with delight, she told me the story—almost as if she knew that she had been part of a secret*

*coup d'etat. The person behind the coup was, of course, Martin de Porres. This is what Doña Paulina told me: "I saved up my pennies over many months and then went over there (she pointed to a clinic for the poor where a statue of Saint Martin de Porres stands quietly in a tiny chapel) to have a talk with 'Martincito.'⁴ I put the coins I had saved at his feet and I said to him, 'Martincito, you know that my sons are far away and that I am too old now to travel to see them. So here, I am leaving this money—enough for your bus ticket. I am begging you to go and bring my sons home to Lima.'" That was it. She did not even ask him to free them from prison. All she asked was that he bring them close to home. She finished her prayers and went back to her newspapers, confident that she had been heard. "And you know what, 'hermanito?' In one week both my sons were transferred to prisons here in Lima." She smiled a huge smile this time, as tears rolled down my cheeks, and as I thought to myself: What I would give to have this kind of faith.*

> The LORD said [to Moses:] "I have observed the misery of
> my people who are in Egypt; I have heard their cry....
> Indeed, I know their sufferings, and I have come down to
> deliver them" (Ex 3:7–8).

## AFFIRMATION OF LOVE, AFFIRMATION OF LIFE

Martin de Porres is very much alive today in the simple, yet profound faith of the poor. He continues to heal the sick and set free the brokenhearted. In him, we glimpse the face of God. In fact, all the saints remind us that our faith is an incarnate faith, and that by looking into the faces of one another, we see Jesus, the human face of God.

As Doña Paulina stood before the statue of Saint Martin, to pray for her two sons, she looked into Martin's compassionate face and trustingly prayed to be heard by the God of unconditional love. Martin smiled on her prayer, and then God answered it. Paulina knows that God answers prayer. Her prayer this time was not only answered, but the answer came wrapped in love.

Once, when asked to define the theology of liberation, Gustavo Gutiérrez, O.P., responded with a question, "How to say to the poor, the oppressed, the insignificant person, 'God loves you?'....This is the question for our Christian commitment.... Ultimately, we have no intellectual answers except to *be with* the poor."[5] Saint Martin is able to communicate God's love so fully, because his life was lived *with* the poor. He heard their cries, he cured their wounds, he embraced them with love. This is what my friend, Doña Paulina, showed me so beautifully as we stood there talking that day on *her* busy street corner in Lima, Peru.

Another great holy person of Latin America, Archbishop Oscar Romero, said in a homily one year before his death, "I simply want to be the builder of a great affirmation, the affirmation of God, who loves us and wants to save us."[6] Today, Saint Martin de Porres continues to live out the *great affirmation of God*, the affirmation of love. He lived it faithfully during his lifetime, and he lives it today in the presence of God, and on behalf of the poor. He lived it by helping to bring Doña Paulina's sons home to Lima. Now it is our turn to be builders of this *great affirmation*, as well.

## REFLECTION QUESTIONS

What does Doña Paulina's faith say to me? How was Saint Martin an instrument of God's love for her? Do I have any favorite saints? Do I approach them with confidence, trusting that through their love I see the face of God? Doña Paulina's prayer was not self-centered. She asked God to allow her to continue bringing the light of Christ's love to her sons. She begged Martin to help her be an apostle of that love. Are my prayers centered on how I might better love others? Who is in need of my prayer *and* my love today? Spend some time in prayer, holding those for whom you pray in the loving presence of your heart.

## NOTES

1. The title *Doña* in Spanish (pronounced *Donya*) is a title of respect, used when speaking to elders and people in authority. The masculine form of the title in *Don*.

2. The Quechua Indians, principally located in the Andean region of Peru, Bolivia, and Ecuador, are still today a very large and vibrant indigenous community, their roots stretching back to the preconquest period. Many Quechuas have migrated the cities over the years in search of work and fleeing from political violence. For most, Spanish is their second language.

3. "Bye, little brother! Have a good day!"

4. The diminutive suffix "ito" is commonly added to words in Peru as a sign of endearment. So *"Martincito"* is translated something like "dear little Martin."

5. Gustavo Gutiérrez, O.P., "An Interview With Gustavo Gutiérrez" by Mev Puleo, St. *Anthony Messenger* (February 1989), p. 10.

6. Archbishop Oscar Romero, *The Church Is All of You*, edited and translated by James R. Brockman, S.J., (Minneapolis: Winston Press, 1984), p. 63. From a homily preached on February 25, 1979.

# Prayer to
# Saint Martin de Porres

To you, Saint Martin de Porres, we prayerfully lift up our hearts filled with serene confidence and devotion. Mindful of your unbounded and helpful charity to all levels of society, and also of your meekness and humility of heart, we offer our petitions to you. Pour out upon our families the precious gifts of your solicitous and generous intercession; show to the people of every race and every color the paths of unity and of justice; implore from our Father in heaven the coming of his kingdom, so that through mutual benevolence in God we may increase the fruits of grace and merit the rewards of eternal life. Amen.

# Bibliography

Alvarez, Guillermo. *Historia de la Orden Dominicana en el Peru*, three vols. Lima: Dominicans of Peru, 1997, 1999.

Busto Duthurburu, Juan Antonio del. *San Martín de Porras*. Lima: Pontificia Universidad Católica del Peru, 1992.

Cavallini, Giuliana. *Saint Martin de Porres: Apostle of Charity*. Rockford, Ill.: TAN Books and Publishers, Inc., 1979.

Clissold, Stephen. *The Saints of South America*. London: Charles Knight & Co. Ltd., 1972.

García-Rivera, Alex. *St. Martin de Porres: The "Little Stories" and the Semiotics of Culture*. New York: Orbis Books, 1995.

Gutiérrez, Gustavo. *Las Casas: In Search of the Poor of Jesus Christ*. New York: Orbis Books, 1993.

Las Casas, Bartolomé de. *History of the Indies*, translated and edited by Andrée Collard. New York: Harper & Row, 1971.

Monahan, Joan. *Martin de Porres: A Saint for Our Time*. New York: Paulist Press, 2002.

Pierce, Brian J. "Martin de Porres: Compassion in Full Bloom," *Justice, Peace & Dominicans: 1216–2001*. Dublin: Dominican Publications, 2001.

Schultz, Bruce B. "Retrieving the African Roots of San Martín de Porras" (unpublished).

Zevallos, Noé. *Rosa de Lima: Compromiso y Contemplación*. Lima: CEP, 1988.